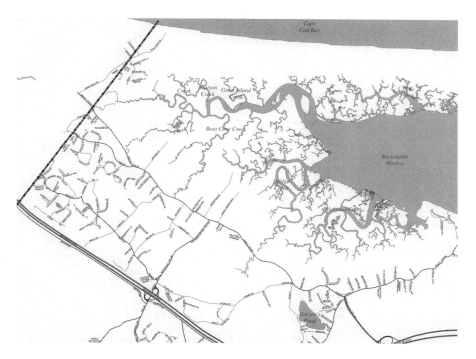

West Barnstable map. *Courtesy of GIS Unit, Town of Barnstable.*

Luminaries of EARLY
WEST BARNSTABLE

THE STORIES OF A CAPE COD VILLAGE

James H. Ellis

Charleston · London

THE
History
PRESS

Published by The History Press
Charleston, SC 29403
www.historypress.net

Copyright © 2014 by James H. Ellis
All rights reserved

First published 2014

Manufactured in the United States

ISBN 978.1.62619.315.4

Library of Congress CIP data applied for.

In memory of a West Barnstable man.

Raymond E. Gilman
PFC, 358th Infantry, 90th Division
August 1, 1915–May 1, 1945

Contents

Preface

In a college criminal law class in Michigan, well before the bicentennial focused renewed attention on the cast of characters in the American Revolution, I listened to the professor give an intense description of a 1761 oral argument in a legal case heard in Boston. The subject at hand was search and seizure, and Professor Houts discussed in detail something called writs of assistance at issue in the Boston hearing. Writs of assistance, despised by the colonists, were general search warrants ruthlessly employed by the Crown's enforcement officers. A young lawyer took up the cause of the Bostonians and presented at trial a lengthy and fiery condemnation of the hated writs. John Adams thought that the presentation sparked the Revolution. Never naming the principal actor and by way of conclusion, the professor asked, "Now, who was the man who argued the case?"

I raised my hand and answered, "James Otis Jr."

Professor Houts appeared stunned, seemingly wondering, "How in the world did that fellow, here in the Midwest, know the answer?" For as long as he had taught the subject, he had always stumped his classes with the question—especially in Michigan, far removed from old Boston. Little did he know that I was born in West Barnstable, half a mile from the birthplace of Otis, arguably the most important or greatest person ever born on Cape Cod and someone not obscure to me.

Later, I told my grandfather Henry A. Ellis about the byplay. He was a prominent Hyannis attorney and an avid student of history. Amused, he responded with a point I thought worth exploring. In his view, apparently no other village in the country outside of West Barnstable made a greater contribution to the nation's early leadership over such a short span of years. In addition to Otis (1725–1783), there was his sister, activist author Mercy Otis Warren (1728–1814); U.S. Navy captain John Percival (1779–1862); and Massachusetts chief justice Lemuel Shaw (1781–1861)—all born in the little village. The New England historian John G. Palfrey at the Barnstable centennial celebration in 1839, in discussing James Otis Jr., narrowed the claim and advanced the contention that outside of the birthplace of George Washington, "No spot in the country has made such a gift to the country, as the spot called Great Marshes"[1] (now West Barnstable). Palfrey's assessment was made without including Percival and Shaw, both in attendance, and their yet-to-be-judged contributions, as well as the merits of the often-overlooked Mercy Otis Warren.

One must keep in mind that West Barnstable is not an incorporated town or municipality. Instead, it is what New Englanders call a village—an informally designated section of a township. West Barnstable is situated in the northwest corner of the town of Barnstable in the middle portion of Cape Cod and is one of seven principal villages in the town. Throughout history, it has been the most rural part of town, and its population in the eighteenth century likely did not match that of other villages in town, such as Barnstable village (the county seat), Hyannis (the up-and-coming business center), Osterville and Cotuit. Part of the reason for its smaller population is the fact it does not have direct access to the sea. The aforementioned four villages were active ports, and in the early years of the country, the ocean served as the highway for commerce and communications. In the first national census in 1790, the entire town reported a total of 2,610 inhabitants. Village breakdowns were not provided. Thus, one can only estimate the West Barnstable population that produced four national, if not international, figures in the half-century period between 1725 and 1781. A fair guess would be less than 500.

I took up my grandfather's challenge, so to speak, and wrote a newspaper piece on West Barnstable's exceptional contributions to the country's leadership and history. But in the back of my mind, it always seemed a subject worthy of a book. In 2014, the Town of Barnstable will hold a yearlong celebration of its 375th anniversary, and this seems as good a time as any to present the West Barnstable chapter of the town's and the nation's story.

Acknowledgements

John Burke of West Barnstable and John Adams of Orleans Camera provided invaluable assistance with the photo and imaging processes, thereby adding a special dimension to this book.

As might be expected with a book on this subject, Sturgis Library of Barnstable and Whelden Memorial Library of West Barnstable contributed a great deal to the necessary research.

Louis Cataldo, the dean of Cape Cod historians, and Tess Korkuch at the Barnstable County–Cataldo Archives added to the work, as did the GIS Unit of the Town of Barnstable and the U.S. National Archives.

As always, my wife, Ruthie, a daughter of West Barnstable, contributed background information, continuous support and editorial help at every step of the way.

The personnel at The History Press—chiefly my commissioning editor, Katie Orlando, and my project editor, Ryan Finn, but also Jeffrey Saraceno—made the end product possible.

To the foregoing, I express my gratitude.

CHAPTER 1

The Great Marshes

In the mid-1800s, Henry David Thoreau thought that development had gotten out of hand in the rural White Mountains of New Hampshire. "I might have supposed that the main attraction of that region, even to citizens," he opined, "lay in its wildness and unlikeness to the city, and yet they make it as much like the city as they can afford to."[2] This kind of criticism has modern application to Cape Cod, an area Thoreau visited and chronicled. He would be appalled by the twenty-first-century reality of a place like the beach at Sandy Neck in West Barnstable, considered in his day to be a "lofty, wild, and fantastical beach."[3] Sandy Neck is a six-mile-long, half-mile-wide dynamic barrier spit shielding the Great Marshes to its south. On summer weekends, its beachfront is overwhelmed with hundreds of recreational camper and sports utility vehicles lined up cheek-by-jowl above the waterline. They come from near and far, dragging along personal watercraft, boats and rafts. Television antennas poke skyward. Flags wave, dogs bark and bonfires glow. The scene is not unlike a World War II invasion beachhead. The beachgoers have carried urban and suburban life on their backs. This is the present state of a prominent natural aspect of the Mid-Cape village of West Barnstable. It did not begin this way.

As much as any New England village, the story of West Barnstable, Massachusetts, springs from its geological past. Remote time explains a great deal. Cape Cod began to take its familiar shape at the end of the last ice age. The final North American ice sheet pushed over the region some twenty thousand years ago. The Laurentide ice sheet moved down from the St.

Sandy Neck northerly view, with Cape Cod Bay in background. *Courtesy of John Burke.*

Sandy Neck southerly view, with West Barnstable village rising in the distance beyond the Great Marshes. *Courtesy of John Burke.*

Lawrence, or Laurentian, area of Canada before melting back or retreating to Baffin Island two thousand years later. The glacier did much work and left in place the basis for the two dominant natural features that would come to define the village in the northwestern quadrant of the colonial town of Barnstable, Massachusetts.

The Laurentide ice sheet had displacement might, carrying everything before it, from massive boulders down to the smallest grains of sand. End moraines made up of this collected material developed along the front margin of the ice. When the ice sheet retreated a second time, it left its massive load along an east-trending belt running the length of the peninsula south of present Cape Cod Bay. Known as the Sandwich moraine, the linear hills of West Barnstable are a part of this geologic leftover.

While the moraine's boulders and stones would impede future farmers, from the earliest time up to the twentieth century, the inhabitants put the material to good use. Wampanoags used the stones to fashion tools and projectile points. Early colonists turned omnipresent stones into building foundations, stone forts, doorsteps and fencing. By the end of the nineteenth century, West Barnstable was covered with stone walls running along roadways, pastures and boundary lines. At the turn of the twentieth century, however, most property owners sold their walls to the town to be crushed and used as base for the paved macadam roads necessary for the growing automobile traffic.

Meltwater streams formed at the edge of the retreating ice sheet. The streams gradually carried silt, sand and gravel downward, creating an outwash plain. At this stage, the landscape in the region was a dry ridge made up of the leavings of the glacier. Sea level was some 110 feet below its present height. Much of the upland of West Barnstable is situated on the outwash plain just below the Sandwich moraine.

As the melting continued apace, the sea level rose, and the Sandy Neck spit began to develop—about 4,000 to 5,000 years ago. Some 3,300 years ago, with the sea level just nineteen feet under the current level, the spit exceeded one mile in length. And by 2,200 years ago, it had taken on an aspect much like the present, assuming a length of more than three miles. When the sea level approximated the modern level, water assumed a primary role in shaping the spit. Ocean waves eroded the highlands of Plymouth, Sagamore and even Scorton to the west, and the prevailing easterly currents carried the sand to Barnstable, where onshore winds drove some of the sand ashore. Continuing winds piled the sand to the south and formed dunes as much as fifty feet in height.

Sandy Neck southwesterly view overlooking the Great Marshes. *Courtesy of John Burke.*

In conjunction with the progression of the spit, the dominant natural feature of the area began to form in the protective lee of the dunes. An extensive salt marsh developed in the bay between the spit and the upland. The marsh is classified as a "high marsh" since it floods infrequently, mainly during some of the periodic high course or spring tides—an important consideration for early inhabitants. Creeks that meander throughout and pools that dot the marsh hold water at all times. A "low marsh," by contrast, floods over as much as twice a day and is not open to as much human use. The vastness—some four square miles—of this Barnstable marsh, which drew the colonists to the place, prompted them to call it the Great Marshes. And for many years, the nearby village—now the Mid-Cape's West Barnstable—was known as Great Marshes.

At this point, it might be helpful to explain the common usage of the names "Upper Cape," "Mid-Cape" and "Lower Cape." In recent years, the terms have engendered much confusion. In early times, residents informally divided the peninsula in two. The Upper Cape consisted of the towns west of Bass River, and the Lower Cape meant all the places to the east of the river. West Barnstable sat in the Upper Cape. Around the beginning of the twentieth century, as Hyannis became the commercial hub of the area, a third division appeared—the Mid-Cape. The towns of Barnstable (including West Barnstable), Yarmouth and Dennis make up this third sector. In the past few decades, a large influx of new arrivals to the Lower Cape fueled another change. Moving to places like Eastham, Wellfleet, Truro and Provincetown, the newcomers could not comprehend how they were lower than towns to the west. Road maps and television weather maps showed their towns higher than the rest of the Cape. Somehow, it all seemed demeaning. A trendy fourth designation resulted. They call their sector the "Outer Cape."

The change demonstrates a total misunderstanding of the original Upper and Lower Cape usage. The terminology is tied to the region's maritime past. The origin is simple, and it does not have anything to do with sailing winds, as some suppose. Generations ago, when marine interests dominated daily activities, places and travel were described in relation to zero or prime meridian in Greenwich, England. To travel east was to move down the longitudinal scale toward zero. To illustrate, a Sandwich–Truro trip is from 70 degrees, 49 minutes, down to about 70 degrees, 5 minutes. Anything to the west of Sandwich was up the scale toward 71 degrees or higher.

To this day, this usage holds firm on Martha's Vineyard. One leaving Chilmark for Edgartown to the east is always going "down island." To return is to go "up island." The phrase "down east Maine" derives from the rule, although many in the Pine Tree State have forgotten or misunderstand their history.

Perhaps the best illustration of the point comes from the western plains in 1856. While attending court in Urbana, Illinois, Abraham Lincoln heard that he had received 110 votes for vice president the day before at the Philadelphia Republican convention. Lincoln's associates reacted with excitement, but he only grinned and said, "Surely it ain't me; there's another great man named Lincoln *down* [emphasis added] in Massachusetts. I reckon it's him."[4] There are other illustrations to explain the usage, but Lincoln makes the case as well as anyone.

While on the subject of geographic nomenclature, a little on the historic names of West Barnstable seems timely. The Indians called the locale *Mos-keeh-tuck-qut*. The name is a compound of *mos-ke-tu-ash*, the word for hay, and *tuck-qut*, a term for navigable water. *Mos* means much. The first comers adopted the literal translation of Great Marshes.

Beginning in 1717, by act of the Province of Massachusetts Bay, along with the rest of the western half of town, the village became the West Parish since it was the seat of one of the two dominant Congregational churches in

Barnstable. As the church lost influence over daily and government life, the current West Barnstable designation gained and held favor.

The English settled the town of Barnstable in the late 1630s and incorporated it as a municipality in 1639. Named after the English borough of Barnstaple in Devon, it has seven principal villages. The term "village" is an informal geographic description without official meaning, although in the early twentieth century, the seven locales formed voting precincts. In addition to West Barnstable, located in the northwest quadrant of the town, there is Barnstable (village), Hyannis, Centerville, Osterville, Cotuit and Marstons Mills. And the villages are carved up further. The best-known example is Hyannis Port—a small section of Hyannis. In the case of West Barnstable, traditionally it is split in two. The western half is referred to as Shark City, while Finntown forms the east.

Describing the outline of West Barnstable can be confusing. The western bound is fixed along the town line of Sandwich. The northern border is static, following the shoreline of Cape Cod Bay. But the eastern and southern lines have varied over the years according to usage or purpose. In yesteryear, most considered the village to be a rather narrow area running close by the old county road (now Route 6A) in the northwestern part of Barnstable. By the 1930s, for voting purposes, the town had labeled the village Precinct 2 and set its lower west to east bound well to the south of the present Route 6A. Recently named Precinct 11, the designation compressed its southern and eastern line inward but included all of uninhabited Sandy Neck. In 1949, West Barnstable established its own fire department or district—the fifth in town.

Thus, in this respect, Barnstable, large in land area, is unique among American municipalities. No other city or town has five separate and independent fire departments. The West Barnstable Fire District lines approximate the old Precinct 2 boundaries. The geographic makeup of the fire districts has more meaning than any of the other designations since the five fire districts tax real estate separately and at different rates. Finally, the federal government got in on the act in 1967 and mandated postal ZIP codes. The West Barnstable, or 02668, code has a boundary that snakes back and forth over the fire district lines and ends up meaninglessly assigning all of Sandy Neck to the village.

The Great Marshes plays an inconsequential role in modern West Barnstable. In the minds of most people today, it is no more than an enormous and passive public conservation area. But in the first three centuries, it more or less defined the village. "As soon as the first settlers came from Europe,

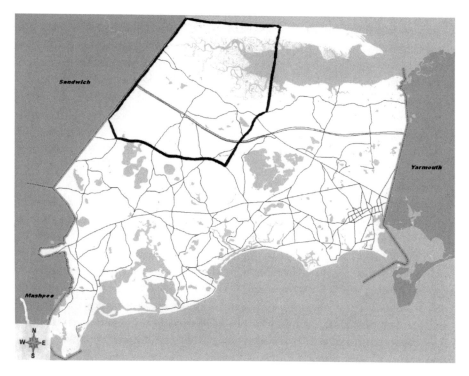

Town of Barnstable map with West Barnstable outlined in the upper-left quadrant. *Courtesy of GIS Unit Town of Barnstable.*

the uncorrupted epoch of the marsh ended...Here was a hay field waiting to be cut."[5] Indeed, the first comers initially called the Barnstable marshes the "Hay Grounds," and the ready and ample availability of fodder and bedding for their livestock and thatch for their roofing prompted them to settle the place instead of the off-Cape location of Sippican.

Barnstable began as proprietary land. The king of England granted the land in the region to a company. In turn, the company granted the land to Plymouth Colony. And the colony subgranted the Barnstable vicinity—or Mattakeese, as it was known—to the settlers of the place. The settlers became the collective owners or proprietors. In effect, the proprietors formed the local government.

At the outset, all the land was held in common. Then, in 1640, the proprietors made the first division, awarding shares or lots to resident individuals. Some land, such as Sandy Neck and the Great Marshes, remained common land, open to all citizens. But in 1696, the proprietors began dividing the Great Marshes among individual proprietors. In 1703, the proprietors made another division of "the upland commons and salt marsh that had not before been divided."[6] Personal ownership that came with division enabled individual management of the parcels.

Modern science judges salt marsh ecosystems to be extremely productive—the ocean's nursery, so to speak. A large percentage of saltwater animals are tied to and depend on the marshes in some fashion at some time in their lives. But the colonists were oblivious to the fact. While they would hunt the plentiful wildfowl present in the marshes, their primary interest was *Spartina patens*, the perennial salt-tolerant cord grass that covered the high marsh. Right away, they found that their feeding cattle and sheep seemed to prefer the marsh grass over fresh upland meadow grasses.

The colonists permitted livestock to graze freely on their holdings. Harvesters started haying late in June and ended in early winter. For the first two hundred years, the men wielded scythes, and twelve-hour days were common. One man recalled, "Mosquitos, gnats and horseflies would sting and bite and bleed me; wet feet and muddy breeches, face burned up like a bun."[7] Late in the 1800s, horse-drawn cutter bars gained favor. Whenever horses worked the marsh, owners outfitted them with special shoe adapters similar to snowshoes. This enabled the animals to walk over the soft surface without sinking. Insects proved a great hindrance to the horses, especially the vicious greenhead flies of July and August. A coat of leather netting thrown over the animals deterred the flies to some degree.

Men gathered and piled the cuttings on staddles. A staddle is a simple circular cluster of wooden posts driven into the marsh, leaving a two- to three-foot portion of each post above ground level. The staddles held the gathered hay in stacks during winds and high course tides until the hay could be carried away in wagons or on barges. The staddles usually served their purpose. They proved a match for the abnormally high tides associated with the Portland Gale of 1898 and the severe northeast gales of early November 1919. But losses occurred. In early January 1886, Thomas Nye lost eight stacks in a storm. A year earlier, a December storm carried away the stacks on thirty or more staddles. Usually the hay was not carted ashore until later in the winter, when the ground was frozen and travel on the marsh became easier. Two pleasant days in January allowed for removal of most of the hay.

Staddles could vary in diameter, but ten feet across seemed common. Each circular grouping contained numerous projecting posts, usually no more than

Unsigned pen and ink on paper entitled *Sandy Neck Hay*, showing a hay staddle of yesteryear. *Private collection.*

a foot and a half apart. Eastern white cedar, red cedar and white oak were preferred for posts, although when the invasive black locust became established in New England, this latter species became the popular source for staddle posts. This wood, some believe, will last fifteen years longer than concrete. Incredibly, although the gathering of salt hay ended in these parts almost a century ago, a few hay staddle posts still poke up from Cape marshes.

The business required relatively little ground preparation, although minimal improvements were made to holdings to enhance the work. The grass grew on its own without encouragement, and it was not plagued by diseases or pests. In the late 1860s, the historian Frederick Freeman found that the Great Marshes annually produced eight thousand tons of hay. When Timothy Dwight visited in the early 1820s, he noted several thousand stacks covering the Great Marshes. By this time, added uses had been found. The hay turned out to be excellent packing for pottery and the like. Icehouse insulation became another use, and the hay turned out to be a fine garden mulch free of weed seeds.

By the late 1800s, the gathering of salt marsh hay in West Barnstable had begun to wane. Within a few decades, the activity disappeared altogether.

In the winter, a few gardeners in the area still pick up hay tossed on shore as flotsam along with other marsh grasses and seaweeds. The gatherings make excellent compost and mulch. But the days of haying on the Great Marshes are in the distant past.

In the mid-1800s, the Great Marshes and Sandy Neck escaped what modern environmentalists would consider an environmental disaster. Led by John Barker Crocker, considered the father of the Barnstable County Agricultural Society, a group planned to dyke the entire marsh. The Great Marsh Dyking, Water Power and Fishing Company, incorporated by the Commonwealth, proposed running a dyke sixteen feet high and fifteen feet wide from upland around Calves Pasture Point north across the harbor to the dunes of Sandy Neck. This line is just to the east and parallel to the traditional West Barnstable boundary with Barnstable village. The scheme intended to keep salt water out "for the purpose of draining the marshes… and converting the same into fresh meadow or tillage land." The corporation also possessed the authority to "raise the water above the dyke, so as to create a *water power*." In addition, the group held exclusive ownership of "any herring or other fishery," including cultivated oysters, which it could nurture behind the dyke. The *Barnstable Patriot* newspaper supported the endeavor and thought that the undertaking also could manufacture ice—"Ice, to be frozen above the dyke, and shipped direct to the South!"[8] All of this would require a pier off the Sandy Neck beach and a railroad running to the pier from the dyke.

The advocates "felt this a magnificent project! Shall we not soon become a Lowell, or a Lawrence? Think of that *'water power.'*"[9] Another suggested benefit was the increased property taxes based on the increased value of the former marshland. The *Patriot* declared that the project "would…in some degree prevent emigration to California from this quarter, and therefore counteract a depopulation which this county appears to be threatened with, and of some of our most enterprising of the community, too."[10] Interestingly, the grand plan was not new. According to its supporters, Colonel James Otis had advanced the idea some one hundred years earlier.

A board of directors consisting of prominent men put together a plan of operations to raise $80,000 by an issue of one thousand shares at $80 each for the purchase of real estate essential to the project. Buyers took up much of the stock, but in the end, the feasibility of the scheme became a problem. As one observer noted, "The rising generation…found it better to leave the marsh mud, and work on solid ground."[11] The project never got underway, and Crocker, the principal proponent, passed on. Nonetheless, as

The Great Marshes looking north near the site of the proposed 1850 dyking scheme. *Private collection.*

late as 1889, the *Patriot* opined, "May some John Barker Crocker, with the disposition and means at hand, rise up in the no distant future, and set the ball in motion which will ultimately make this vast now almost waste land the most productive in the country."[12]

In addition to haying and dyking, men found other uses for the marsh. Duck hunting became a major draw. At the pinnacle of wildfowling (late 1800s–early 1900s), gunners considered the Barnstable marsh one of the premier duck hunting spots in the world. Speaking generally, in 1895, a writer observed that "there is probably no more favored locality than Cape Cod" for duck gunning.[13] Hunters targeted the American black duck (*Anas rubripes*), although they did not overlook geese, other puddle ducks, sea ducks and shorebirds. Sportsmen came from afar and retained the services of local guides. Local gunners earned a large share of their livelihood by shooting birds for market. Hunting camps, or "shanties," popped up all along the shore, especially on Sandy Neck, and a craftsman designed a special duck boat for the locale. "This craft is indigenous to Cape Cod's Barnstable

Marsh," a sportswriter reported, "where it is employed with deadly results by the native gunners and the shooters from the city who go out with them. The Barnstable boat is flatbottomed, with a covered foredeck and a cockpit amidships girdled with a coaming to keep out the slop in rough weather. It slides over mud like a toboggan, floats on a moderate dew, and is amazingly seaworthy for such a low-slung craft."[14]

Duck hunting declined rapidly after World War II, and the sport is just about nonexistent on the Great Marshes at present. Nobody expects the glory days to return.

During almost the same period, a more valuable natural resource existed for the taking in the Great Marshes and contiguous Barnstable Harbor. Tracing to earliest times, soft-shell clams (*Mya arenaria*), quahogs (*Venus mercenaraia*) and razor clams (*Enis arcatus*) prevailed in great abundance. An 1841 state report found the supply exhaustless. At the time of the report, soft-shell clams were used mainly as bait in the cod and haddock fishery. Shippers sent great quantities to Boston for this purpose. While almost all of the marsh is within West Barnstable, just about the entire associated harbor is in Barnstable village. The shellfish flats are situated in both places. Since both are in the town of Barnstable, the distinction means little. The town exercises regulatory control over clamming.

The historian Henry Kittredge considered the 1910–25 period to be the peak of Barnstable clamming. He recalled the tidal flats dotted with clammers and their dories, to the great consternation of the duck hunters. Diggers worked in teams, often three men to a dory. The object was to fill the dory on a single tide. Digging proved to be backbreaking work. The record seems to be ten barrels dug by one man on one tide. The term "tide" as used here refers to that three-hour or so daytime period when the water is out and the flats are more or less dry. The soft-shell clam is intertidal—that is, the animal lives in bottom ground that is under water except at low tide. This explains why the common but incomplete expression "happy as a clam" originated as "happy as a clam at high tide."

Clams were so plentiful and profitable in 1925 that the board of selectmen approved a year-round open season. Within two years, things began to get out of hand, and restrictions appeared. The selectmen saw the folly of their lenity. They prohibited Sunday clamming. Barnstable clams brought six dollars per barrel, "the highest price paid for clams in New England…and we can't half supply the demand," said an interested fisherman. He wrote to the *Patriot* editor explaining the Sunday ban. The man noted that 50 to 125 men dig clams in the harbor when it is

Sandy Neck easterly view, with Barnstable Harbor in the distance. *Courtesy of John Burke.*

open. Each is permitted one barrel per day. "I dare not say how many thousands of dollars have been taken out of Barnstable Harbor in the last 16 months," he reported. "It is not to be wondered at that private interests are always trying to grab all they can get away with."[15]

The correspondent stressed the harm done to the industry by "out-of-town people, who have no interest excepting to trim our flats of all they can get...The second Sunday in November of last year there were 96 people from out of town taking scallops and clams for their own use, as well as for the use of their uncles, aunts, brothers and grandmothers." The following Sunday "there were 127 all bent on the same object."[16] The situation deteriorated to the point that selectmen prohibited all clamming for trade in the harbor from April 1, 1928, to the end of the year.

Nonetheless, things got worse. In the latter part of 1930, the clam warden reported that "the diggers this year...have stripped the harbor of almost every clam of the most desirable size with the result none are left for next year." He continued, saying, "There has practically been no set [seed deposit] at all for the past five years and if even there should be a good one this coming year it will take several years for the clams to grow to the desired size."[17]

The shellfishery made something of a recovery, and during the Great Depression, clamming afforded many Barnstable men their only source of income. Presently, shellfishing in the marsh and harbor pales in comparison to earlier times. Comparatively few wild shellfish exist, so the town government stocks cultivated quahogs and oysters for recreational shellfishers. At the head of the major creek leading out of the Great Marshes, a number of grantees grow quahogs and oysters for sale. In a program started in 1906 and emphasized in recent years, a fairly sizeable area is set aside for this kind of cultivation. At the turn of this century, fifty shellfish grants covered a block of one hundred acres. For a fee, grantees exercise complete control over their grant parcels.

Dyking, the virtual disappearance of wildfowl and the collapse of the Barnstable shellfishery would have been considered disappointing if not catastrophic to the first residents of these parts—the People of the First Light.

CHAPTER 2

People of the First Light

An early chronicler concluded that Massasoit, the chief sachem of the Wampanoag tribe of southeastern Massachusetts and parts of Rhode Island, "held dominion over divers other petty sagamores" [sachems] on Cape Cod and the islands.[18] From this, the historian Frederick Freeman concluded, "The Indians upon the Cape were not considered as a part of the Wampanoag tribe, whatever may have been their position in regard to Massasoit." They were "made up of distinct tribes."[19] For the most part, the Freeman distinction no longer is made. Those who occupied the Cape before the coming of the English in the seventeenth century are regarded as Easterners, People of the First Light and People of the Dawn or by the native name Wampanoags.

The Indians who inhabited much of the West Barnstable locale appear to have been seasonal occupiers of the land. Proof does not seem to exist showing a permanent native settlement of any size in the village proper. In fact, when Gookin in 1792 reported on the progress of the gospel in these parts, he found relatively small settlements in the northeast, southeast and southwest quadrants of Barnstable, but nothing in West Barnstable. The nearest settlements were to either side. The celebrated Cummaquid sachem Iyanough located his band in the northeast section of Barnstable while overlapping part of West Barnstable. The Aquetnet settlement under Sea-qu-unks was situated at Skauton, or Scorton Neck, and held sway into Barnstable to include much of the Great Marshes. However, there remains considerable evidence that Wampanoags spent much time at Sandy Neck—mainly, it appears, in the warmer months.

Distant view of one of the larger middens, or shell heaps, in the interior of Sandy Neck. *Courtesy of John Burke.*

Intermediate view of the midden. *Courtesy of John Burke.*

Close-up of the same midden. *Courtesy of John Burke.*

Colonial history places the Indians resident on the Neck in the summer but not in the winter.

Confirmation of early residency takes the form of aboriginal artifacts left during the Woodland period (sometime between 1000 BC and AD 1600). Cultural traits common to the period include small, defined territories; bow and arrow use refined; use of resources from inlets of the sea (fish, mollusks and so on); use of pottery; semipermanent villages; and saplings driven in the ground as part of shelter construction. A number of past archaeological studies document evidence of this kind of early behavior on Sandy Neck. Indeed, even today, an untrained eye can discover corroboration.

Edward Brooks from 1932 to 1935 conducted an early study of the shell heaps (middens) on Sandy Neck. Aided by Ripley P. Bullen, he published his findings in a 1948 bulletin of the Massachusetts Archaeological Society. In one midden, he found oyster shells in the lower section, while the top part of the heap contained a mixture of scallop, soft-shell clam, sea clam, razor clam, quahog and mussel shells. Anyone hiking through the dunes at present would not have difficulty spotting one or more of these ancient piles. The dunes are exceedingly dynamic, changing from storm to storm, so middens can be in sight today and gone tomorrow. Generally, they appear at blowouts cleared by the winds. At other times, wind-driven sands accumulate and obscure all signs of a given pile.

Brooks also found many pottery shards about the heaps. Sandy Neck tradition represents that some time ago, late in a day, a saunterer spotted a number of prehistoric clay pots high on a dune. He decided to return in the following daylight and gather his find. But during the night, a strong blow ravaged the dune, hiding the pottery altogether. Yet a sharp-eyed hiker today can spot any number of small pieces of ancient ceramics, usually of a buff, tan or brown color.

More common are lithics, or stone artifacts, especially flakes, chips and spalls left over from the production of arrowheads or projectile points. This debris tends to be found in concentrations, suggesting the location of a work station. From time to time, "turtles," or blank arrowheads, crop up. Turtles are roughed-out or incomplete points that have a profile similar to the shelled reptile. Of course, completed arrowheads are most prized. Often they are found in near-perfect condition away from the work sites, suggesting use in hunting game animals. Once buried by wind-blown sand, a point or arrowhead remains preserved and unchanged until uncovered altogether by following winds. A point can remain under the sand for centuries and thus protected.

The ample cobble deposits on the beachfront attracted Wampanoags to Sandy Neck. After gathering a supply of siltstones, silicates and indurated shales, the men retired to the protection of the dunes and went about the task of fashioning tools, especially the common arrowhead. They carried their work product with them when they returned to the upland at the end of the season, leaving chips scattered about.

A second report of note appeared in 1967 after Bernard W. Powell traversed the Neck over three days in the summer of 1965. His archaeological study supported the findings of Brooks and added another interesting aspect. About the shell heaps, he found a number of sharpened wooden butts up to six inches in length, cut to a point at one end and rotted down at the top end. Powell suggested that the butts "may be terminal ends of saplings or posts driven in [by Indians] for temporary fire screens, windbreaks, drying racks, or perhaps even lodges or wickiups."[20] Powell acknowledged that his theory was open to challenge, but he was impressed with the fact that he found most of the butts close to the middens.

A third survey worth mentioning took place in 1992. The Barnstable Historical Commission retained Fred Dunford and Doug Erickson to conduct a search for archaeological sites on the Neck. As much as anything, the town's interest stemmed from the fact that it owns about 95 percent

A private camp on Sandy Neck next to the trail along the Great Marshes. *Private collection.*

of Sandy Neck. In the 1600s, the place rated as common or public lands. Over time, private interests took over. Throughout much of the last century, the municipality reacquired most of the land. The threat of development prompted this effort. At one point, a proposal surfaced to pave a roadway the length of the spit. There remain about two dozen camps stretched along the marsh side. A few are wholly private. Some are private buildings on leased public land, and the rest are altogether publicly owned and leased. At the tip, there is a private colony of about a dozen cottages along with an inactive lighthouse. Four-wheel-drive vehicles are required to access these places. At any rate, the Dunford effort confirmed the work of Brooks and Powell and lamented the fact that over time, identified sites have been disturbed by collectors and others.

Amateur interest in the shell heaps, though regrettable, is understandable. Occasionally, remarkable finds are reported. An 1884 discovery piqued more than a little interest. In one of the major middens discussed at length by Brooks and the following two investigations, several Cape men found six silver coins of Spanish origin dating to the period between 1721 and 1782. "The finding establishes the fact conclusively," the local newspaper reported, "that the coins in question were obtained by the Indians from the whites, through traffic or otherwise, provided the locality was occupied as an encampment or abiding place of the Indians only."[21] In addition, the men found a rare copper arrowhead in a nearby heap. This discovery presumes the copper came from the English or from a western tribe.

While the Sandy Neck middens were magnets for early arrowhead hunters, up to the mid-twentieth century spent arrowheads were scattered in relative abundance throughout West Barnstable and the rest of the Cape. Thoreau, an avid artifact collector and admirer of the native peoples, makes the point. In one of his trips to the Cape, he described the profusion of arrowheads. When at High Head, he said, "I picked up half a dozen arrow-heads, and in an hour or two could have filled my pockets with them."[22] Two generations ago, when open farmland dominated the village of West Barnstable, arrowheads were fairly easy to find. Freshly turned ground, especially if followed by an early season rain, prompted numerous men and boys to poke around in search of the projectiles. The farms have disappeared, and most of the upland is overgrown. Yet observant gardeners from time to time still uncover arrowheads in their little plots.

While on the topic of Sandy Neck relics, it may serve to shift to more recent times. Anyone walking the Neck today in search of Wampanoag artifacts can spot more modern signs of human intervention. While the colonists treated the place as a valuable asset to their agricultural, fishing and whaling pursuits, by the late nineteenth century, some viewed the peninsula as an expansive wasteland open to abuse. In 1896, the 4th U.S. Artillery marched down to Barnstable from Fort Adams in Newport, Rhode Island. The men set up their cannons on Calves Pasture Point and blasted away at targets two and a half miles away on the Neck. Four years later, Battery A came down from Boston, set its cannons in a field behind Ellsworth Howland's house and fired on targets 2,500 yards to the north in the dunes. "Some excellent work was done by the men with a large crowd of onlookers to admire their skill."[23] Shrapnel from these exercises can be uncovered today.

After the Great War, in 1921, field artillery units of the Massachusetts National Guard revived the gunnery practice. They set up at various points along the Great Marshes and in the uplands of West Barnstable and shelled the Neck with full charges. When the Guard returned the following summer for a planned two-month encampment, locals felt that enough was enough. In August, the Cape Cod Chamber of Commerce asked the adjutant general to discontinue the disruptive and hazardous activity.

The plea began by indicating that the artillery practice "is coincident with the active season for summer visitors." Also, the projectiles crossed over "a

A collection of Indian arrowheads and projectile points gathered in the West Barnstable vicinity. *Courtesy of John Burke.*

navigable waterway leading from Barnstable harbor to West Barnstable used by fishermen, pleasure boats and gunners…The explosive shells also pass over and sometimes fall upon a town road," as well as the public beach. The chamber added, "The town owns a portion of the back beach and erected a bathhouse for public use, but it was shot to pieces last year and has not been reerected." Continuing, it noted, "There seems to be an impression amongst your officers…that…you were simply using waste or common lands, and were not, as you are, infringing the rights of private owners and the rights and safety of the public on waterways and public roads." In conclusion, the protest declared, "The camp itself is undesirable and a handicap to the community…[M]en wander widely at night, the majority are well behaved, but the result is to attract to the Cape an undesirable element." While asking for a discontinuance of the encampment, the chamber made a veiled threat of legal action.[24]

The protest generated an unacceptable response, causing the Cape business group to send another letter to Guard headquarters in Boston. "The commanding officer," the chamber felt, "seems to treat our respectful protest with petulant impatience." The officer denied any trespass or property destruction. So, the chamber furnished some details. In the middle of the summer, "an artillery battery was wantonly driven three times through the peach and apple orchards of Ivar Pelton [on Oak Street] in West Barnstable, resulting in the killing or serious damage of thirty young peach trees and three apple trees. The actual damage was settled for by the payment by the commonwealth of $250 to Ivar Pelton on August 29th." The letter concluded, "The range is only made safe by the arbitrary and unlawful exclusion of the public from the beach and waterways, and the private owners from their property."[25]

Another exchange of correspondence followed, treating the subject of live ordnance. The Guard claimed that "every shell fired has been seen to explode." But the Cape protestors replied, "On July 24th while hunting for Indian relics on Sandy Neck," an East Sandwich man "found on the sand dunes between the inside and outside beach a 3-inch (?) unexploded shell."[26] After this back and forth, when the next season rolled around, the Guard decided to practice elsewhere. But to this day, shell fragments from the 1921–22 cannonading appear from time to time in the windswept sand dunes.

The military returned to Sandy Neck during World War II and again left its mark. The place became a bombing range. Army and navy fighter bombers dropped MK-23 iron training bombs on improvised targets in the dunes, usually empty metal barrels. Most often, empty oil drums served as targets. Now rusted, some of the barrels remain visible today. The devices were not highly explosive, armed only with a ten-gauge shotgun shell, and everything that did not break apart upon impact was collected by souvenir hunters years ago. Broken pieces, however, remain scattered about. The army also positioned antiaircraft guns on the Neck during the war and fired on targets towed behind low-flying planes operating out of nearby Camp Edwards. Infantry units likewise conducted spirited maneuvers on the Neck during the duration.

This period also spawned one of the more intriguing and unresolved Sandy Neck mysteries, a tale worth a passing mention. During World War II, a former German officer from the previous war found his way from New Jersey to the Neck. He took up residence in one of the camps along the marsh trail and lived a solitary and somewhat secretive life. Suddenly, when the war ended in 1945, he disappeared. A few years later, a local youngster stumbled on a cache of nitroglycerin behind the camp occupied by the German. The state police detonated the unexplained explosive material on site, shaking the north side of town. Although there is no evidence that the

A rusting barrel target on Sandy Neck left over from World War II bombing practice.
Courtesy of John Burke.

man did anything untoward during his stay, these few facts gave rise to a legend—the German spy or saboteur of Sandy Neck.

Modern military activity contrasts sharply with the initial intrusion on Indian lands in the area. In 1637, Englishmen began settling in the north of what is now the town of Barnstable. They found the Indians pacific; in fact, in the first winter, they received much-needed aid and shelter from the original inhabitants. The Plymouth Colony took note of the interest in the locale and granted land for official settlement to one Richard Collicut. Known as Mattakeese by the natives, the grant covered the area along present Barnstable Harbor and extended part of the way into present West Barnstable. Collicut failed to settle, so the authorities at Plymouth voided his grant and issued a second to Thomas Dimmock, Joseph Hull and their associates. This group took up the land but soon yearned for more.

Indians were the nominal owners of large tracts of coveted acreage. So, under the colony's supervision and with its consent, the settlers went about dealing with the owners. In 1641, a small piece of land to the east of Mattakeese went for the price of "one dwelling house, wth a chamber flored with bord, wth a chimney and an ouen therein."[27] What is erroneously called the First Purchase followed in 1644, and it took up almost all of the

The commemorative marker placed in 1939 at the site of the Crocker fortification house off Church Street. *Courtesy of John Burke.*

future West Barnstable and more. Sea-qu-unks (often referred to as Serunk) received four coats and three axes for the large parcel. Three other major purchases, the last in 1664, followed to complete the town's makeup.

From the outset, relations between the newcomers to Barnstable and the original inhabitants proved friendly. Nonetheless, threatening incidents elsewhere involving Indians created apprehension throughout the colonies. In 1642, Plymouth and Massachusetts Bay entered into a mutual defense agreement. Barnstable enrolled thirty-two men to serve in a regiment headed by Captain Myles Standish.

The initial scare subsided, but Plymouth authorities took note that Barnstable did not provide fortifications for its people. Accordingly, in 1643, Plymouth ordered the town to "forthwith appoint a place or places for their defense and to cause the same to be speedily fortified for their defense." In response, the three church deacons—Dimmock, Henry Cobb and William Crocker—set about to "provide for the personal safety as well as the spiritual wants of the people."[28] For the purpose, they constructed twenty-five-feet-square houses of two stories with steep roofs. The outer walls of the lower floors were made of the omnipresent fieldstone left by the prehistoric glacier, while hewn logs were used for the top floors. The second floors formed an overhang above the first, and they included loopholes to permit shooting guns outward. Internal cisterns provided water. Crocker located his "fort" in a West Barnstable field just to the north of the western end of the present Church Street. The structure had been taken down by the early 1800s. During the tercentenary in 1939, the town placed a memorial tablet at the site. Like so much of the village, in recent decades, the spot became wildly overgrown, and consequently, it is unfamiliar to most residents.

The town remained on edge, even though the Indian neighbors, unlike others in the colonies, continued their peaceful ways. When in 1675 the vicious King Philip's War broke out nearby in the region, tranquility prevailed on the Cape. However, required to participate, Barnstable sent its share of men to battle off-Cape and suffered its commensurate share of the losses. In the sanguinary Rehoboth battle of March 26, 1676, also known as Pierce's Fight, six Barnstable men fell. Lieutenant Samuel Fuller, Samuel Bourman, Samuel Childs, Eleazer Clapp, John Lewis and Samuel Linnell are at the head of the long list of native sons who throughout the centuries gave the last full measure of devotion.

CHAPTER 3

The First Comers

Cape folklore advances the theory that an intense storm prevented Barnstable from becoming America's hometown instead of Plymouth. After landing at what became Provincetown, Massachusetts, the Pilgrims in early December 1620 set out to find a better place to locate. A party sailed its shallop westerly along the shore of Cape Cod Bay, then Stuards Bay. When in the vicinity of the entrance to Barnstable Harbor, a violent snowstorm and rainstorm supposedly obscured their view of the entrance to this otherwise attractive harbor, and they continued on to the next major inlet at Plymouth. This fanciful speculation draws on William Bradford's description of the trip. While moving along the north shore of the Cape, he wrote that the discovery party "discerned no place likely for harbor; & therefore hasted to a place that their pillote, (one Mr. Coppin who had bine in ye cuntrie before) did assure them was a good harbor."[29] Coppin had his sights set on Plymouth, known as Thievish Harbor since a native stole a harpoon from English whalers at the place sometime in the past.

Of course, the area was not terra incognita to at least the *Mayflower* officers. Verrazzano cruised these waters as early as 1524, followed by Gosnold in 1602, Weymouth in 1605 and Champlain in 1608. In fact, the latter mapped Plymouth Harbor in 1608. Captain John Smith followed by mapping the entire coast from Cape Cod to the Penobscot River in 1614. Barnstable Harbor was not unknown. As much as foreknowledge, the Pilgrims could look across the bay from windswept Provincetown and see the alluring hills of Plymouth. Another seventeen years would pass before the English moved to settle what became Barnstable and West Barnstable.

"First comers" or "old comers" are names referring to the earliest English settlers in Plymouth and the nearby colonies. The colonizing of West Barnstable is tied to and flows from the initial settlement just to the east in the present village of Barnstable. Some of the first comers to neighboring Barnstable village became the first Englishmen to soon thereafter drift westerly and take root at the Great Marshes.

Before Richard Collicut's 1637 grant to settle in the area then known as Mattakeese, unrecorded forerunners looked over the vicinity. When Collicut failed to establish habitation, the Plymouth Colony Court revoked his personal rights but permitted other individual occupants acting under his grant to remain in place. Reverend Stephen Batchiler and a small band from Lynn occupied the area in the winter of 1637–38 but left after a few months. A year later, in March, Thomas Dimmock of Dorchester moved in, followed in May by Reverend Joseph Hull of Weymouth. Both remained under the Collicut permit. Within a few months, the two men and their followers erected primitive dwellings. Authorities did not make a confirmatory deed or grant to cover all of this until July 1685.

The official beginning of the town is hazy. The month and day of Barnstable's incorporation remains questionable, although the year, 1639, is accepted. The historian Amos Otis sets the date as June 14, when the colony appointed a Barnstable constable, William Casely. A later historian, Charles F. Swift, takes issue and argues that the correct day is December 3, when Dimmock and Hull received appointment as deputies to the General Court. Henry Kittredge adopts the December date. Writing in 1794, Reverend John Mellen set the date as September 3 without explanation. Probably because early September is a seasonable time to celebrate, in 1839 the town's bicentennial committee picked the Mellen date while offering a weak rationalization for doing so. Historian Simeon Deyo sided with the committee. Adding to the confusion, in 1970, the Commonwealth put out a monograph declaring the incorporation date as March 5, the day Plymouth instructed Dimmock to train the men of his settlement in firearms. This order seems to be the first time the name "Barnstable" appears in official records. Donald Trayser correctly recognizes that "the exact date…[of the year] can never be positively known."[30] The uncertainty stems from gaps in the early records, as well as the fact that the earliest towns in Massachusetts were not incorporated de jure, by formal charter, but in practice, or de facto.

In the scheme of things, October 21, 1639, may be a more important Barnstable date than any associated with incorporation. On that day, Reverend John Lothrop, followed by some two dozen families, arrived from Scituate. This group turned out to be the heart of early Barnstable. A pious man, Lothrop received his education at Christ College, Cambridge, England. He settled in a ministry outside London but, after five years, renounced his holy orders. Separated from the Church of England, he found his way to London and in 1624 succeeded Reverend Henry Jacob as pastor of the Congregationalist Society in the city.

Ten years later, Lothrop arrived in Massachusetts and located in Scituate. The community established a church, and the members elected him pastor. After several years, the group turned its eyes toward Barnstable and its vast salt marshes. With Lothrop in the lead, families with surnames forever associated with Cape Cod—Baker, Bearse, Cobb, Crocker, Davis, Hinckley, Lewis, Mayo, Scudder and the like—made their way to Barnstable. The Hamblen family also made the trek. A less common name on the Cape today, citizens throughout the nation knew the name 150 years ago. A direct descendant of the Barnstable Hamblens, Hannibal Hamlin of Maine served as Lincoln's first vice president.

Lothrop's arrival along with a number of his followers signaled the end for Reverend Hull. The little settlement did not have room for two ministers. Of the two, the more talented Lothrop appealed to a majority. Hull shifted to neighboring Yarmouth. The Barnstable church excommunicated him in May 1641, and before long, he left the Cape for New Hampshire.

Since Lothrop prevailed over Hull and remained at the head of the local church until his death in 1653, his name is more often associated with an old Barnstable relic. At the outset, the people worshiped outdoors in good weather and otherwise in individual homes until the town erected a meetinghouse in 1646. Long-held tradition places many of these early gatherings at and on a large glacial erratic known as "Sacrament Rock," located where the roadway now passes in front of the current Barnstable–West Barnstable elementary school and almost on the nebulous line between the two villages. Lothrop is said to have administered the sacraments and preached his first sermons from the spot. The town held some of its first civic meetings at the site, then called the "Great Rock" or the "Town Rock."

The rock stood on a bluff on the south side of the roadway. In 1820, workers cut off a substantial piece and used it for the foundation of a new jail. Undermined by storm runoff, in about 1870 the town considered the remainder a hazard and rolled it across the street. In time, road crews

Sacrament Rock along the Old King's Highway at the Barnstable–West Barnstable village line. *Courtesy of John Burke.*

broke it up and used the pieces to level a widened highway. In 1916, the local newspaper noted that the rock "is not gone beyond recall."[31] A town committee formed, collected some of the fragments and pieced them together to create a stone-like memorial that stands today almost unnoticed on the north side of the highway.

After giving thanks to the Prince of Salvation, the first comers set about dividing the land. Most of the entries in the town records of the seventeenth century deal with land or property matters. As one example, "under date ye 20th of 3d mo 1640 that no Inhabitant within this Plantation shall make sale of his house or any of his land, before he hath offered it to ye inhabitants and in case ye Plantation buy it, then to provide a purchaser whome ye town shall approve."[32] This tendency of critically passing judgment on newcomers to the Cape became deeply ingrained in the collective psyche of the place. Over the centuries, Cape Codders have considered transplants to the peninsula to be different if not lesser. Things did not change until the latter part of the twentieth century, when people from away became the majority. Even then, to suggest that they possessed a special connection to the maritime heritage of the Cape and were deserving of acceptance, in recent years, new arrivals began to call themselves "washashores."

In any case, for the first century, land occupied the attention of the town fathers. They appointed land measurers, supervised fences, laid out and divided common meadows, managed Sandy Neck, provided land for a community fulling mill, regulated cattle (especially on common lands), set aside sites for fish houses and try yards and tended to scores of related tasks.

Before they got a handle on land matters, the original settlers concentrated on the critical task of constructing shelter. Many of the initial dwellings tended to be crude, no more than one-room shanties. They generally used hewn or hand-sawed planking and sealed the cracks with local clay. Instead of glass windows, oiled paper covered openings. Stones formed the foundations and were utilized in the construction of chimneys. Thatch from the salt marshes served as roofing. Lothrop indicated the simplicity of the design by referring to some of these structures as "booths."

A sawmill operated in Scituate and produced lumber for the colonies. Over time, bricks and diamond glass windows became available. Men of some means purchased these materials and within just a few years refined and expanded their dwellings, adding one room at a time. A typical improved house measured about twenty-two by twenty-six feet and consisted of one and a half stories. The family lived in a "great room," usually located in the southeast or sunny corner. The kitchen occupied the northwest corner, while a pantry took up the northeast corner above a cellar. Placed in the remaining corner, a fireplace could be as large as four feet in depth and eight feet in width. The part that formed the oven often projected out of the side of the house. This prompted one wag to knock on the door of such a dwelling and inform the lady therein, "Madam, do you know your oven has got out of doors?"

She replied, "Will you have the kindness to bring it in, it is too hot for me to handle?"[33]

Even as improvements followed, the elements could be a challenge. An early Barnstable physician adopted a rule not unlike the Chinese of the period, who measured cold by the number of jackets worn. "He had on his bed a dozen all-wool, fulled blankets. In the summer he turned down one or two." As fall progressed, "he turned down three or four, and during the coldest weather in winter he buried himself under the whole. With him the weather was from one to ten blankets cold."[34]

While the desire to worship God in their own way motivated the first to arrive in town, they felt that making money was equally important. Stock

A herd of cows in the north of Barnstable in about 1968—a common scene in 1640 but now vanished. *Private collection.*

farming initially produced the most profitable results. From 1630 to 1640, it was the most lucrative business in the colonies. Numerous farmers in England sent over cattle, placing them for half the profit. "A record of the sale of four two-year-old steers and a bull, which were wintered" in Barnstable in 1639–40, set the price paid at eighty-three pounds, "an enormous sum, considering the value of money at that time."[35]

The migrants from Scituate found the limited meadows in that town too crowded in the summers, and fodder proved scarce in the winter since it was impossible to grow sufficient grain in the largely wooded terrain. They appreciated the boundless Great Marshes and its ready hay, as well as large upland fields opened up by the Wampanoags, and they followed in the footsteps of Hull, already busy raising cattle at Mattakeese. The business required little if any capital, and a man of small means could enter. However, after just a few years, prices in the market plummeted, along with the hopes of fortune. The large-scale raising of cattle and other livestock for gain declined on the Cape.

Along with the market fall, wolves turned out to be a problem. The colony paid a bounty on the predators, but they persisted. In 1654, stalkers shot or trapped nineteen in total, three in Barnstable. A year later, colonists killed thirty-one, with nine falling in Barnstable. The problem continued. Hunters overall killed thirteen in 1690 and nineteen one year later. Wolf Neck jutted into the upper reaches of the marsh in West Barnstable, so named since wolves favored the spot. Joseph Bodfish almost lost his life there while tending his traps. Finding a large wolf in one of his traps, he struck the animal in the head with a pine branch. The aroused and angered beast lunged, breaking the trap chain. An agile Bodfish jumped aside and escaped before the stunned animal could fully recover. His grateful family preserved the trap as an heirloom.

Bodfish continued to hunt the cursed brutes and developed a keen knowledge of his quarry. Sometime after his escape on Wolf Neck, a team of hunters asked him to join in pursuit of a wolf the men had chased to Barnstable from Wareham. Drawing on his understanding of the habits of the animal, he declined but took up his gun. Knowing that the wolf would come back as he went, Bodfish assumed a stand along the path. In due time, the pursued retraced its steps, with fatal consequences. Soon after Bodfish returned to his house, the Wareham hunters showed up and said that they had lost the track of the wolf in Yarmouth. The men felt awkward when Bodfish produced the carcass of their prey.

As late as 1717, a local man by the name of Garret received a bounty of nine pounds for killing a wolf. But one year later, the town suspended the wolf bounty program. By 1734, birds had become the problem. Barnstable required all men married or single and at least twenty-four years old, "except aged, infirm, ministers & school-masters," to annually kill four mature crows, blackbirds or blue jays or pay a fine of nine pounds.[36]

Dividing the land, building shelter, stock farming and pest control did not take up all of the time of the old comers. Domestic issues were front and center for many. Large families produced independence and wealth for the times. By their mid-teens, boys could do the farm work of a man. Girls, of course, helped their mothers with household chores, from cooking to

Bodfish Farm, West Barnstable, in 1967—now extinct but the site of some housing. *Private collection.*

weaving. The belief of the time held that the birth of a son increased a man's wealth by one hundred pounds and a girl added fifty pounds. Tax records support the point. Men who paid the greatest taxes headed the largest and usually most influential families.

Women were as important and managed to have their say in family matters. A young lady by the name of Grace offers a romantic example. A farmer's daughter, she grew up helping her father in the fields and became proficient with the sickle. Two men sought her hand in marriage. The parties agreed that the fellow who could reap the largest section of field in an allotted time would gain the nod. The field was marked off in three equal sections, with the middle lane given to Miss Grace. "She was the best reaper, and having decided that she would marry Thomas Hatch, she slyly cut over on the part set off to him, and in consequence Thomas came out ahead, claimed and received her hand in marriage."[37]

By and large, the Barnstable first comers tended to be intelligent, and many were well educated. After matters of faith, their second most important consideration involved the education of their children. John May, one of Lothrop's band, held the specific title of teaching elder as early as 1639. In 1670, Plymouth Colony set up a mechanism to fund free education through the profits of the fisheries off the Cape-tip. Barnstable received fishery money in 1682 and established one of the first five schools in the colony.

All things considered, the first comers to the West Barnstable area enjoyed a relatively good life. Subsistence farming provided many necessities— vegetables, grains, dairy products, poultry, pork, mutton and the like. People produced their own wool, flax and leather. Hunting contributed game, and seafood existed for the taking. Firewood was plentiful. Some items, such as peas and fish, were sold off-Cape, and the earnings were saved to purchase manufactures from England or the larger towns of the colonies. Only loafers and laggards found the going rough.

After the first wave of settlers from elsewhere, many years passed before meaningful numbers of people moved to the town. The population, nonetheless, grew at a steady pace, and talk turned to the need to divide the town in two.

CHAPTER 4
West Parish Separates

An Irishman took the first formal step in the creation of a distinct identity for West Barnstable. Richard Coote, First Earl of Bellomont, is not a familiar name to modern New Englanders. A member of the British Parliament, he backed William of Orange in the Glorious Revolution of 1688. In 1695, the incumbent governor of Massachusetts Bay, Sir William Phips, died. King William III and Queen Mary II commissioned their supporter Bellomont to succeed Phips as governor of Massachusetts, as well as of the New Hampshire and New York provinces.

Bellomont arrived in Boston in May 1699. His tenure turned out to be brief. Just days before his death, in February 1700, the governor ordered the town of Barnstable divided in half on a north–south line for military purposes. Captain John Gorham received command of the 1st Foot Company, formed in the east, and Captain John Otis became head of the 2nd Foot Company in the west. Heretofore, the little settlements scattered throughout town were treated as one and serviced by a single meetinghouse, located next to Coggins Pond just about midway between Mattakeese and Great Marshes and close to Sacrament Rock.

As the new century progressed and the population spread throughout town, the need for a civic division received increased attention. The necessity of two meetinghouses and two religious societies occupied the attention of many. In January 1713, a town meeting provided for the appointment of a twelve-member committee to study the issue. "[A]fter much discussion and deliberation," an October 1715 meeting advanced the issue, followed by a meeting one year later that found unanimous sentiment to divide.[38]

Barnstable required the approval of the Province of Massachusetts Bay before it could act on the matter. In its petition to the General Court, the town indicated that the remoteness of the single meetinghouse to some residents prompted the request, adding that a regularly warned meeting unanimously agreed to two societies. On October 24, 1717, another meeting settled on a north–south dividing line running along the western shore of Nine Mile Pond (now Wequaquet Lake) and proposed by a five-member special committee. The court approved and declared, "[E]ach Precinct may be enabled to Act by & for themselves…& have full Power to raise Money by Way of Rate in each Precinct apart for Building & Repairing Meeting Houses & Settling & Maintaining Ministers."[39]

The internal division stands out since it became the only statutory division of any sort in Barnstable history. The other three early Cape towns underwent downsizing partitions. The town of Bourne split from Sandwich. Dennis separated from Yarmouth, and Wellfleet and Orleans left Eastham. Later, Brewster left Harwich.

Anticipating the action of the town meeting and the General Court, two dozen men in the east end of town got a head start. A year before final approval of the division, and without authority, they set about constructing a new meetinghouse on Cobb's Hill in the middle of what would become the East Parish.

In 1711, Jonathan Russell Jr. succeeded his deceased father as Barnstable's minister. When appointed, the town made it clear to young Russell that "ye settling and ordaining of him shall be no obstruction to ye church and Town Either to ye Calling of another Minister to assist… or to become two societys when we can unanimously agree to either of them."[40] Nonetheless, Russell objected to the new construction and its implications and protested to an Ecclesiastical Council made up of pastors and delegates from out-of-town churches. The council found that each side of the controversy displayed "too much heat" and served "rather to exasperate each other's spirit than to cultivate peace and love."[41] While the council condemned the unconformable action of the apologetic builders, it suggested acceptance of their work.

This left the West Parish in need of a meetinghouse. A three-man committee bent to the task and selected a site in the approximate center of West Barnstable. Construction began in 1717 and took close to two years to complete.

A pencil sketch of the West Parish meetinghouse by Rebecca W. Crocker in about 1840. *Private collection.*

Now it was time for Russell to choose to remain in the new East Parish or remove to the new West Parish in West Barnstable. In August 1719, he explained that "through divers accounts it seems most natural for me to abide in the precinct where I now am; yet since there is such a number who are so prejudiced or disaffected and so sett against my being there; as yt my life is likely there to be rendered less comfortable to me," he decided to pick the "Western Settlement."[42] In the church records, Russell noted that "the first of my preaching in the West meeting was on Thanksgiving day Nov. 1719."[43]

When Russell moved to the West Parish, he carried along the core of the original church—records, sacramental vessels of pewter and communion silver. This led to immediate controversy and promoted a questionable and long-lasting narrative. The East Parish thought that it was entitled to half the silver. Courteous pleadings failed to move the West Parish. When the East threatened to seek relief from an Ecclesiastical Council, the West relented and gave up two of four communion vessels of silver. The records and pewter were not treated.

As for the lasting issue, first, it is essential to clarify the traditional meaning of the words *church* and *meetinghouse*. In the present as well as in the past, *church* refers to the body politic, the society. *Meetinghouse* means just that—a place to hold meetings, whether religious or civic. The meetinghouses of the early period were public buildings supported by local taxes. This remained the case in Massachusetts until 1834. Thereafter, it became acceptable and common to call the structure as well as the society a church. Be this as it may, a doubtful categorization of the society's place in history has promoted a myth about the meetinghouse's standing. A commonly advanced claim of the present asserts that the West Parish meetinghouse is the oldest Congregational house of worship in the country. This assertion traces to a misunderstanding of an earlier pretention that the church is the direct continuation of the first Congregational church society formed in Southwark, London, England, in 1616 by Reverend Henry Jacob and, therefore, is the oldest Congregational church in the world.

Local history everywhere is sprinkled with dubious and exaggerated claims. Descriptions of things of the past liberally resort to superlatives such as "first," "earliest," "oldest," "biggest" and the like. The frank advice of a Harriet Beecher Stowe character who felt it imperative to "contrive allers [always] to keep jest the happy medium between truth and falsehood" seems to guide many.[44] The practice is not limited to casual conversation. On the Cape, venerated institutions gild the lily with apparent ease. For one of many examples, the Cape Cod Baseball League, tracing to an early West Barnstable ball game, claims an establishment date of 1885 knowing full well that there is absolutely no basis for the arbitrary date. The earliest supportable year is 1923, and that may be a stretch. As a second illustration, the Falmouth Historical Society possesses an antique marine cannon that it proudly claims comes from the town's War of 1812 nemesis, the HMS *Nimrod*. Accessible and conclusive evidence shows that the pretension is nonsense.

The West Barnstable church is caught up in a similar web. Reverend Hiram Carlton, pastor from 1853 to 1862, gave the issue life. Carlton, drawing on early writers, argued that the church was, in fact, the continuation of the first church in London, initially removed to Scituate with Reverend Lothrop and thence to West Barnstable by way of Barnstable. Lothrop, of course, while in England succeeded Henry Jacob, the founder of the Southwark church. The Carlton supposition falls apart when it is noted that Lothrop was dismissed from the London church before he came to New England as a private person. The church was not broken up and did not remove to Scituate with him. It continued for a time in London. Therefore, the West Barnstable church is no more than an offshoot of the original, just as Lothrop's Scituate and Barnstable churches were before. Eminent historians such as Henry Kittredge, Amos Otis and Charles F. Swift are among those who have questioned, if not debunked, this continuing claim of originality.

The persistence of the Carlton conjecture led to the belief that the meetinghouse outdates all others of its kind. Talk of the oldest church induces some who do not appreciate the church-meetinghouse distinction to believe that the structure is the oldest Congregational building. Semantics are always in play, but two essentially Congregational church buildings in Massachusetts are older than the substantially restored West Barnstable building. Hingham's Old Ship Church dates to 1681, and the Old Indian Meeting House in Mashpee goes back to 1684. A Yale professor considered the 1712 Newington, New Hampshire meetinghouse to be "the oldest building of the Congregational denomination in the United States."[45]

This kind of adornment and embellishment is unnecessary. The West Barnstable church and the meetinghouse, especially, are historically important regardless of their ranking among counterparts. In fact, the old meetinghouse has come to characterize modern West Barnstable.

In any event, following the division, the population of the West Parish continued to increase. In just four years, it became necessary to enlarge the meetinghouse. Carpenters cut the building in half and pulled it apart

An 1892 view of the West Barnstable church after the 1852 modernization. *Private collection.*

by eighteen feet. An addition filled the gap. While on the project, the men added a tower on the north end. To top it off, the parish purchased a gilded cock weathervane from England. The symbol traces back in Christianity to Saint Peter and remains in place after almost three hundred years. In 1852, the building underwent a major modernization, greatly changing its outward appearance. By 1950, the meetinghouse had fallen into disrepair. A movement began to restore the structure to its early 1723 form. Work started in 1953, and it was more or less completed by 1957.

Maintenance of the minister received much public attention in the West Parish during the early eighteenth century. Town meeting appropriations supported his annual salary. Other necessities, such as firewood, were

Left: The gilded cock weathervane from England that was placed on the meetinghouse at an early date. *Private collection.*

Below: The West Parish meetinghouse or church after the restoration of the 1950s. *Private collection.*

contributed by townsmen. Typically, a dozen or so men were assigned the task of providing from one to three cords apiece. The week following Thanksgiving was usually set aside as the time to get up the wood. In 1700, the elder Reverend Russell became apprehensive when September rolled around and he did not have his supply. He found it necessary to make a formal request "for his fire wood…having formerly…been encouraged by principal inhabitants to expect it."[46]

The meetinghouse itself became the focal point of the village. The town schoolmaster, or the minister himself, used the facility as a schoolhouse. Many but not all town meetings were held in the West meetinghouse. Stormy proceedings became the norm. After a century of heated and sometimes physically destructive meetings, the need for a civic gathering place became apparent. The *Patriot* newspaper led the movement. An 1830 editorial wondered, "[W]hat consistency can there be in using a building dedicated to the exclusive purpose of the worship of the Almighty, to assemble men to finish business where all the worst passions of human nature are called into action[?]" Editor S. B. Phinney added, "We seriously wish that our religious societies would be as obstinate as some that we knew of Worcester County, where neither party would yield an inch, and one town meeting was actually held under a shed of [a] barn, and that on a wet, rainy day."[47] Seven years later, Major Phinney saw his goal achieved. Barnstable constructed a town house for civic gatherings in the geographic center of the town, equally inconvenient to all.

In the early years of the parish, Sunday services also could be less than tranquil. In August 1724, Justice of the Peace Daniel Parker issued an order to the West Parish constables and tything men to "suppress Revelling, Sporting and rowdy behavior" at the meetinghouse. (Tything, or tithing, men were parish officers assigned to preserve order during services and generally enforce the observance of the Sabbath.) Parker indicated "as well from my own observation as by the Information and complaint of Divers other sober Persons tis evident that the Sabbath Day is wickedly, shamfully and Publickly Profained and that at the Place of Publick worship especially before and between meetings to the great dishonor of God Almighty." Parker targeted "young Persons Chiefly (tho its to be wished that Persons of more mature years would sett better examples…than they do)." He noted that the miscreants "come to the meeting house before the Publick Worship begins and spend time Chiefly in Revelling Sporting and Playing and make the assembly but a meer Rout as If that was the business they come upon." The crowd turned the place "into a den of Theifes…a sad omen of the great decay of Religion amoung us." He instructed the recipients of his order to repair to the meetinghouse as early as possible to "prevent and suppress all Rudness Noysey Talking disorderly and unbecoming behaviour which is unseemly at that time and place." If warranted, the constables or tything men could "moderately correct" the "gilty." But if "any Person or Persons shall appear to be Turbulent & ungoverned or incorragable," they were to be reported to Parker "or some other of his Majts. Justices of the Peace."[48]

The outcome of Parker's policing effort is unrecorded. But it is safe to surmise that some semblance of order prevailed before too many months passed. A year later, singing within the service itself became the central issue. Some parishioners wanted to sing the "old way" (one line at a time). Younger members preferred the "regular way." The dispute continued until December 1726, when the congregation agreed to sing the old way for six months and the regular way for the other half. Reverend Russell noted, "During the half year we sang the old way the singing was very broken and confused, Bro. Bodfish setting the Psalm."[49] The parish consequently returned to the regular way, and a council supported the method in a 1729 ruling.

While all of this change and commotion transpired about the meetinghouse, an ordinary event with great implications took place at the Otis homestead along the shores of the Great Marshes just to the west of Bridge Creek. On February 5, 1725, Colonel James Otis and his wife, Mary, celebrated the birth of the second of their thirteen children. They named him James Otis Jr.

CHAPTER 5

James Otis the Patriot

By 1725, the Otises of West Barnstable stood as one of the leading families in the colony. A sketch of their accomplishments explains. General John Otis started things in this country. Born in Barnstaple, England, in 1581, he arrived in Hingham, Massachusetts, in 1635 along with his son, John. The younger John spent time in Barnstable before moving back to the South Shore and Scituate. He left a son on the Cape— the third man bearing the name John. Continuing, the latter also fathered a son John, who came to be known as Colonel John.

As a sign of things to come, townsmen appreciated Colonel John because of his "distinguished talents…powerful wit, great affability, sagacity, prudence and piety."[50] He commanded the county militia for eighteen years, served in the legislature for two decades, sat as first judge of probate for more than a dozen years and was chief justice of the Court of Common Pleas for twenty-one years. True to form, he had a son John, as well as a sixth child and fourth son named James, born on June 14, 1702, in West Barnstable.

Colonel John's namesake John came to outrank his father, attaining the grade of general in the militia. He also served as a representative and council member for nine years and as king's attorney for a period. Nathaniel, the second of the colonel's sons, was register of probate for a number of years. The third son, Solomon, held the positions of register of deeds and county treasurer.

The youngest son, James, outdid his siblings. Unable to pursue a classical education as did the two older brothers, he relied on the "native energy of his mind."[51] John Adams took note of this overall characteristic. "'He is vastly good humored and sociable,' Adams wrote. 'Learned he is not.'"[52] A tanner by training, James seemed to stumble into the legal field. He happened to be at the Barnstable Courthouse when a friend found himself in immediate need of legal aid. The man asked Otis to serve as his counselor. Otis accepted the challenge and won the case. This success prompted him to learn the profession through home study. After a year of plunging into law books, he appeared at the Superior Court and took the oath as an attorney.

Over time, Otis became a militia colonel and member of the legislature, serving as Speaker of the House for two years. James also served as judge of probate and chief justice of the Court of Common Pleas. "After being many times negatived by the royal Governors, he was chosen and confirmed as a member of the Council, and from the departure of Gage [1775] to the adoption of the State constitution [1780], by virtue of being the senior member of the body, he exercised during that period the functions of chief executive magistrate of Massachusetts."[53]

Consistent with the lifestyle of the period, James and Mary (Allyne) raised ten children. The parents named their second and oldest child to survive infancy James. In later years, to distinguish the two men, the public referred to the elder as Colonel Otis. When the son's contribution to the birth of the nation became appreciated, he became characterized as James Otis the Patriot. His devoted biographer believed that "before the year 1770, no American, Dr. Franklin only excepted, was so much known, and so often named in the other colonies, and in England."[54]

Colonel Otis regretted his lack of a college education and vowed that things would be different for his offspring. He placed his son James under the preparatory tutelage of the local minister, Reverend Jonathan Russell Jr. Young Otis entered Harvard in June 1739 and received a bachelor's degree four years later. The record suggests that he did not exhibit a dedication to his studies until exposed to the Great Awakening. The eloquent and passionate George Whitefield, a touring English revivalist, spoke in Boston in 1740. He made a deep impression on Harvard students, including Otis. The experience appeared to prompt Otis to immerse himself in his studies. Later, he adopted aspects of Whitefield's oratorical style. In 1746, Otis earned a master's from the Cambridge college, but years later, he lamented the fact that he did not spend more time studying science and the humanities before moving on to jurisprudence. Otis considered general life experience a valuable preparation for the legal profession. In a letter home to his father, he expressed support of his younger brother Samuel's course of broad scholarship prior to taking up the study of law.

Jeremiah Gridley, a preeminent Boston lawyer, tutored Otis in the field. Upon being admitted to the bar, Otis moved to Plymouth and established a law practice. But the minimal challenge of the small community did not match his superior talents. Within two years, he returned to Boston and built his reputation. An early case spread his name throughout the colonies and beyond. Three merchants charged with piracy in the Admiralty Court in Halifax, Nova Scotia, paid a remarkably high fee for his services. When Otis secured acquittals for the trio, he secured his standing with the public.

Adversaries spoke highly of the man as a lawyer. Loyalist Thomas Hutchinson, governor of the Province of Massachusetts Bay twice during the 1760–74 period and a political opponent, remarked on his character as an attorney. Hutchinson thought "he never knew fairer or more noble conduct in a pleader than in Otis; that he always disdained to take advantage of any clerical error or similar inadvertence, but passed over minor points, and defended his causes solely on their broad and substantial foundations."[55] This is a remarkable assessment when it is realized that since his time, the American practice of law has more or less devolved into a search for error.

Sadness shadowed the man's marriage. In early 1755, he married Ruth Cunningham, daughter of a prosperous Boston merchant. Described as beautiful, gentle and refined, she possessed a handsome dowry along with Tory sympathies. The contrast with the passionate genius and intense rebelliousness of her husband, however, led to more than a few curtain lectures. "Nevertheless," Otis "in his serene moments always professed an affection for his Ruthie."[56] Two of their three children became sources of early anguish in the family. Their son James III, an ensign in the Continental navy, died on a British prison ship in 1777. Almost as disheartening for the father, their daughter Betsy married British army lieutenant Leonard Brown a few months after he survived wounds at the 1775 Battle of Bunker Hill. The couple removed to Sleaford, Lincolnshire, England, another bitter pill for Otis. Their third child, Mary, proved less disconcerting. She married the son of American major general Benjamin Lincoln. The general is notable for having received the sword of surrender at Yorktown from British general Charles O'Hara, acting in behalf of Lord Cornwallis.

Before long, Otis became a leader in the Boston bar, specializing in mercantile and admiralty issues. He represented leading merchant families such as the Hancocks, Hulls and Vassals. At the same time, he turned to classical literary pursuits. He published a study titled *The Rudiments of Latin Prosody*, and he prepared a similar manuscript on the rhythmic and

Statue of James Otis Jr. on the lawn of the Superior Courthouse, Barnstable. *Courtesy of John Burke.*

intonational aspects of the Greek language. This affection for classical studies served him well in times to follow.

As young Otis became active in the legal and political circles, it must be appreciated that his father already operated at the top levels. Many considered the senior Otis the nominal head of the Massachusetts bar. In 1748, he received the appointment of province attorney general. In 1762, just as political differences between the Crown and the province were heating up, the General Court elected the elder Otis to the influential Massachusetts Council. The father wound up playing a major supporting role in his son's mercurial career.

From the earliest days of the American colonies, the great distance from controlling authority in London acted to promote independent behavior on the part of the colonists. As an early example, in 1644, the governor of Massachusetts and the governor of French Acadia unilaterally agreed to a peace and free trade pact. Massachusetts did not seek approval from England but instead went to the united colonies of New England (Plymouth, Connecticut and New Haven in addition to Massachusetts) for ratification. At first, the king and British Parliament paid little attention to the trend several thousand miles removed. However, when the colonies became thriving entities, London began to expect dutiful obedience. The colonists resisted all moves to curtail their de facto independence while agreeing that they were Crown subjects bound by the laws of England.

The outcome of the French and Indian War (1754–63) affected London's approach to governing the American colonies. British military victories in North America culminated with the September 1760 conquest of Montreal. Most fighting on the continent ended at this point, enabling Great Britain to focus attention on problems arising from the self-reliant tendencies of the colonies. Issues of taxation and revenue were at the forefront. John Marshall, the future chief justice of the United States, in an understatement summarized the result in his history, observing that "a considerable degree of ill humour was manifested in Massachusetts with respect to the manner in which the laws of trade were executed."[57]

At the time, James Otis Jr. occupied the lucrative post of acting advocate general, or chief prosecuting attorney of the Admiralty Court in Boston. Immediate events propelled Otis to the highlight of his career. Although he would continue to make major contributions to the popular cause, his actions over a few months in 1761 gained him lasting fame and placed him in the select circle of heroic Founding Fathers. The eminent historian John Clark Ridpath thought that five or six men headed the list of great "early

American prophets." He placed Benjamin Franklin in the top spot. "After him it was difficult to name a second." He offered Thomas Jefferson, Samuel Adams, Thomas Paine, Patrick Henry and James Otis as possibilities.[58]

The authorities started a campaign of strict enforcement of Parliament's trade regulatory laws. Thomas Hutchinson, then lieutenant governor of Massachusetts, became a principal in the unfolding drama when in November 1760 he accepted the position of chief justice of the Superior Court at Boston. Charles Paxton, surveyor and searcher of His Majesty's customs in the port of Boston, applied for a writ of assistance or general search warrant. Sixty-three merchants, many of them among the most prominent members of the community, objected in a lawsuit. The customs authorities expected that Otis would aid in presenting their case in support of issuance of the writ. But he detested the odious implications of the document and resigned his advocate general post, moving to the other side as co-counsel along with another leading lawyer, Oxenbridge Thacher. Indicative of the intensity of his beliefs, Otis took up the merchants' case pro bono, asserting that "in such a cause, I despise all fees."[59]

The resignation of Otis gave rise to the persistent and unsupported charge that he was retaliating against the government that disappointed his father. When the Superior Court chief justiceship became vacant in the fall of 1760, many expected that the elder Otis would gain the position. Arguing against writs of assistance was presumed to be a way to revenge the family's blighted hope. Any review of the facts refutes this foul claim. *Quincy's Reports* cited immediately here presents such an exploration. More important, this document may be the best single source on the subject of writs of assistance, providing more historical and legal detail than most will need.

The writ sought by Paxton directed all sheriffs, justices of the peace and constables to assist him and his deputies. Among other related powers, the writ authorized Paxton "to enter & go into the vaults cellars warehouses shops & other places where any prohibited goods wares or merchandizes or any goods wares or merchandizes for which the customs or other duties shall not have been duly & truly satisfied and paid lye concealed or are suspected to be concealed, according to the true intent of the law to inspect & oversee & search for the said goods wares & merchandize."[60] Needless to say, such a broad grant of arbitrary and discretionary power would not be considered in Massachusetts and the United States today, largely because of the thinking of Otis that forms the basis of the Fourteenth Article of the Massachusetts Bill of Rights and the Fourth Amendment prohibitions against unreasonable searches and seizures.

The first argument on the Paxton case took place in February 1761 in the Boston Town House (now Old State House), with Chief Justice Hutchinson presiding over a panel of five. Jeremiah Gridley, later assisted by Robert Auchmuty, appeared for the government. Auchmuty had assumed the advocate general post vacated by Otis. A second argument took place in the August term of the court, and the decision was handed down in mid-November. The February hearing, however, proved the most important and remarkable, with Otis at his rhetorical best. Gridley, the attorney general, opened with a justification for issuance of a writ. Thacher responded with a contrary technical presentation. Then "Otis spoke and lifted the question to a different level, in one of the memorable speeches in political history."[61] What we know of the words of Otis come from the scant notes of John Adams, not yet a member of the bar but an attendee, as well as his perhaps embellished written recollections years later. The younger Adams was a protégé and admirer of Otis. In his early effort to start his career, Adams "fashioned his behavior and professional style" after his mentor.[62] Adams confided in his diary, "I find myself imitating Otis."[63] There are shortcomings to the Adams notes and remembrances, but they make up the only purported account of the argument of Otis.

Adams recalled that Gridley "argued with his characteristic learning ingenuity, and dignity, and said everything that could be said in favor" of the petition for a writ, "all depending, however, on the 'if the Parliament of Great Britain is the sovereign legislature of all the British empire.'" Thacher followed "and argued with the softness of manners, the ingenuity and cool reasoning, which were remarkable in his amiable character." "But Otis was a flame of fire!—with a promptitude of classical allusions, a depth of research, a rapid summary of historical events and dates, a profusion of legal authorities, a prophetic glance of his eye into futurity, and a torrent of impetuous eloquence, he hurried away every thing before him." Adams concluded, "American independence was then and there born...Every man of a crowded audience appeared to me to go away, as I did, ready to take arms against writs of assistance. Then and there was the first scene of the first act of opposition to the arbitrary claims of Great Britain. Then and there the child Independence was born."[64]

Gridley and Thacher had completed their arguments by two o'clock in the afternoon. Otis took more than four hours to present his position. He opened declaring, "I will to my dying day oppose with all the powers and faculties God has given me, all such instruments of slavery on the one hand, and villainy on the other, as this writ of assistance is." Otis argued, "It appears to me the worst instrument of arbitrary power, the most destructive

Portrait of James Otis
Jr. after a painting by
Joseph Blackburn and
an engraving by Oliver
Pelton. *Private collection.*

of English liberty and the fundamental principles of law, that ever was found in an English law book."[65]

Otis recognized the magnitude and consequences of his challenge. "I shall not think much of my pains in this cause, as I engaged in it from principle…I have been charged with desertion from my office. To this charge I can give a very sufficient answer. I renounced that office, and I argue this cause from the same principle; and I argue it with the greater pleasure, as it is in favour of British liberty, at a time when we hear the greatest monarch upon earth declaring from his throne…that the privileges of his people are dearer to him than the most valuable prerogatives of his crown; and it is in opposition to a kind of power, the exercise of which in former periods of English history, cost one King of England his head, and another his throne." He also acknowledged, "Let the consequences be what they will, I am determined to proceed. The only principles of public conduct, that are worthy of a gentleman or as man, are to sacrifice estate, ease, health, and applause, and even life, to the sacred calls of his country."[66]

He then proceeded to the matter of the writ. Otis agreed that the old law books on justices of the peace contained general search warrants for houses. But, he emphasized, the modern books include only special warrants to search specific houses based on sworn suspicion. A general warrant is illegal, he argued, and it "places the liberty of every man in the hands of every petty officer." Thus, "I deny that the writ now prayed for can be granted" since in "the first place the writ is universal, being directed 'to all singular Justices, Sheriffs, Constables, and all other officers and subjects'…Every one with this writ may be a tyrant in a legal manner, also may control, imprison, or murder any one within the realm." Next, "[I]t is perpetual, there is no return." Thirdly, one armed with this writ may enter in the daytime "all houses, shops &c. at will." And fourthly, "[B]y this writ not only deputies, &c. but even their menial servants, are allowed to lord it over us." He ended this phase of his argument with a fundamental precept that is deeply imbedded in English liberty, tracing to 1567, and familiar today. "A man's house is his castle," he said, "and whilst he is quiet, he is as well guarded as a prince in his castle. This writ, if it should be declared legal, would totally annihilate this privilege."[67]

Otis then presented anecdotes to move his argument. He said that a Mr. Pew had one of these writs, and when a Mr. Ware succeeded him, Pew endorsed the writ over to Ware. A court did not have the chance to judge the suitability of Ware. And Ware thereafter found himself appearing before Justice Walley, charged with profane swearing on the Sabbath. "As soon as he had finished," Otis continued, "Mr. Ware asked him if he had done. He replied, Yes. Well then, said Mr. Ware, I will shew you a little of my power. I command you to permit me to search your house for uncustomed goods; and went on to search the house from the garret to the cellar; and then served the constable in the same manner!"[68]

Since the statute authorized any person a writ, Otis declared, "Every man prompted by revenge, ill humour, or wantonness to inspect the inside of his neighbour's house, may get a writ of assistance. Others will ask it from self-defence; one arbitrary exertion will provoke another, until society be involved in tumult and in blood."[69]

Adams reported that Otis then presented a "dissertation on the rights of man in a state of nature…His right to his life, his liberty, no created being could rightfully contest…[H]e sported upon this topic with so much wit and humour, and at the same time with so much indisputable truth and reason, that he was not less entertaining than instructive. He asserted, that these rights were inherent and inalienable. That they never could be surrendered or alienated, but by ideots or madmen, and all the acts of ideots and lunatics were void, and not obligatory, by all the laws of God and man."[70]

Otis concluded his argument with an extensive examination of the acts of trade, and "one by one...demonstrated," as Adams recalled, "that if they were considered as revenue laws, they destroyed all our security of property, liberty, and life, every right of nature, and the English constitution, and the charter of the province."[71] Before he ended, Otis offered the prescient observation that "if the King of Great Britain in person were encamped on Boston Common, at the head of twenty thousand men, with all his navy on our coast, he would not be able to execute these laws. They would be resisted or eluded."[72]

Over the years, many in addition to Adams have applauded the Otis speech. Daniel Webster thought, "Unquestionably, that was a masterly performance."[73] George Bancroft called it "the opening scene of American resistance."[74] Albert Bushnell Hart and Edward Channing together declared, "James Otis's speech...is conveniently regarded as the first in the chain of events which led directly and irresistibly to revolution and independence. It marks the tone of public opinion in Massachusetts in 1761."[75] And A.J. Langguth concluded, "James Otis stood up to speak, and something profound changed in America."[76]

In the end, the eloquence of Otis did not turn the Crown. After the second argument and at the conclusion of the August term, the justices immediately and unanimously ruled in favor of Paxton and the writs. The court adjourned on November 19, and the customs officer had his writ by December 2. While Otis lost the cause at hand, his effort served a greater purpose. The days and years to follow would make this clear.

After the first writs argument, Otis's repute was without bounds. According to Adams, his speech "secured him a commanding popularity with the friends of their country, and the terror and vengeance of her enemies; neither of which ever deserted him."[77] In the May 1761 election, the men of Boston elected him one of their representatives in the General Court. This prompted Loyalist and soon-to-be-appointed chief justice of the Court of Common Pleas Timothy Ruggles to lament at dinner at Colonel John Chandler's Worcester home, "Out of this election will arise a damned faction, which will shake this province to its foundation."[78]

Ruggles, of course, proved prophetic. Otis seemed to be spoiling for a fight. When the General Court went back in session late in the fall of 1761, it took up Governor Francis Bernard's call for action on the problem of counterfeiting. The matter soon turned to a dispute over sound money

James Otis Jr. memorial stone, placed by the Sons of the Revolution in 1917 along the highway near the site of the Otis homestead. *Private collection.*

versus cheap money. Hutchinson and the Council favored the former, and Otis and the House supported the latter. The Otis position on this difficult subject appealed to agrarian and debtor discontent. Hutchinson wanted to devalue gold to a correct relationship with the supposedly invariable silver standard. When the legislative session ended without a solution, the parties took to the newspapers to push their views and attack one another. Otis considered Hutchinson's actions a personal challenge, and Otis taunted his adversary in print. This response, "a combination of vicious satire, legalistic argument, and common sense," became typical of the man.[79] Hutchinson wrote to a friend, "The town is full of contention."[80]

When the legislature returned in 1762, it passed an act making gold legal tender and dealt with the issuance of notes of the province. The legislators ignored the counterfeiting issue. In the end, the currency controversy, as much as anything, seemed to be no more than a means for Otis to go after his nemesis Hutchinson and the government party.

As the currency dust-up faded, Otis remained alert for an opportunity to defend the common man and popular rights. Governor Bernard provided an opening when he unilaterally funded the outfitting of a province ship to patrol in support of Massachusetts fishermen. While the outlay did not amount to much, Otis saw it as an affront to the legislature's responsibility for approving appropriations and a move toward unaccountable autocratic rule. Bernard agreed in general but prorogued the General Court to put an end to the issue. Otis would not let the matter die. He wrote a fifty-three-page paper entitled *Vindication of the Conduct of the House of Representatives of the Province of Massachusetts-Bay*. The essay became "one of the most widely read early statements of the fundamental principles of American revolutionary theory."[81]

Otis continued his pamphleteering. In early 1764, Parliament passed and the king's commissioners signed the so-called Sugar Act, a law levying a direct tax on the colonies. A plain point of contention arose, and Otis took note in a tract titled *Rights of the British Colonies Asserted and Proved*. In brief, he acknowledged the general supremacy of Parliament, but he disputed the notion that it had the right "to impose duties and taxes upon a people, who are not represented in the House of Commons."[82] Both sides accused him of disloyalty. Yet the central theme—taxation without representation—became the rallying cry of the eventual independence movement.

A dispute in Rhode Island opened the way for another Otis essay of note. Rhode Island governor Stephen Hopkins became embroiled in a contentious exchange with Loyalist politician Martin Howard. Since Howard was an outspoken critic of Otis, it did not take much for the latter to enter the fray behind the governor. Howard responded in kind, prompting Otis to write a retort called *Brief Remarks on the Defense of the Halifax Libel*. One historian considered Otis's effort "one of the best examples of a genre of the times—the partisan, invective-filled personal attack, bursting with uncontrolled self-righteous anger and aimed at unsettling the opponent while allowing one's followers to read along with vicarious enjoyment."[83]

The next issue to receive Otis's attention proved much more consequential. The *Rights* pamphlet aroused and incensed many in London. As a response, in 1765, Parliament imposed a direct tax on the American colonies requiring much printed matter to use British paper with embossed revenue stamps. Again, the taxation-without-representation question took center stage. The Stamp Act appeared in Boston in May as Otis launched a campaign against the measure. He, like many of the key figures on both sides of the running debate, took to the newsprint. By December, pieces submitted by Otis usually appeared under the pseudonym "John Hampden." Hampden, of course, was the heroic seventeenth-century Whig politician in England who challenged

King Charles II. The newspaper debates caused Bernard to consider Otis "as wicked a man as lives."[84]

Within just a few weeks, feelings rose to a fever pitch in Boston, and violence seemed inevitable. Andrew Oliver, a stamp commissioner, became the first target. In mid-August, an unruly mob destroyed his shed, thought to be associated with his government duties. The throng then proceeded to Oliver's home and wrecked his house. Hutchinson, present at the time, fled along with the commissioner. All of this proved sufficient to prompt Oliver to resign his post. The mob moved on to stone the lieutenant governor's house. The sheriff told Hutchinson that he did not command the resources needed to disperse the mob. A fortnight later, following much agitation in town, the rabble reappeared at Hutchinson's place and proceeded to loot and destroy his North End dwelling. In addition to valuable private property, Hutchinson lost many government records and much documentation that he had gathered as material for a history of the province.

Loyalists blamed the violence on Otis. Governor Bernard claimed, "Over this junto Mr. Otis deservedly presides, and, by his superior powers of inflaming and distracting an infatuated people, is become the director of the whole."[85] Evidence, however, shows that the tumult disgusted Otis. At a special town meeting on the following day, Otis passionately urged civility.

Otis looked for a solution. As a leader in the legislature, he proposed a meeting of committees from all of the colonial legislatures. As a result of his efforts, a number of the colonies, including nine of the original thirteen American colonies, met in October as the Stamp Act Congress. Sometimes called the First Congress of the American Colonies, the group gathered in New York intent on a unified protest against an arbitrary Parliament. Recognized as the heart of the gathering, Otis represented Massachusetts as part of a three-man delegation. In the end, the Congress adopted a *Declaration of Rights and Grievances*, as well as several lesser petitions. London more or less ignored the position papers. However, Caesar Rodney, a Delaware delegate and later a signer of the Declaration of Independence, recalled, "It was this Congress, in which James Otis, of Boston, displayed that light and knowledge of the interests of America, which, shining like a sun, lit up those stars that shone on this subject afterwards."[86]

After much anguish on the part of Bernard and his loyal followers and continued racket from Otis and the popular party, word of the repeal of the Stamp Act reached Boston in April 1766. The government in London tried to downplay the groundswell of opposition in the colonies and rationalized that a downturn in the economy prompted the repeal.

In the spring election, Boston returned Otis to the House, and the members promptly elected him Speaker, subject to Bernard's approval. While the repeal of the Stamp Act set the stage for reconciliation all around, the governor could not tolerate the thought of Otis in the chair. Bernard sent a note to the General Court indicating his rejection of Otis. The disapproval produced an unintended result. The ranks of the opposition popular party increased and united, with Otis informally at its head.

A few months of relative quiet preceded the next issue: the hated Townshend Acts. Chancellor of the Exchequer Charles Townshend gained 1767 passage in Parliament of a series of laws that again levied taxes on the American colonies. He wanted funds to pay the salaries of governors and judges without going through the self-willed colonial legislatures. As well, he perceived a need to pay for troops to maintain the peace in the colonies. The taxation-without-representation dispute reappeared. In response, Otis and Samuel Adams joined together in early 1768 and wrote a so-called Circular Letter on behalf of the Massachusetts House. In brief, the letter, sent to the other colonies, asserted that the acts in question were unconstitutional and contrary to natural law. The king was not amused, and his government ordered Massachusetts to rescind the "rash and hasty" letter.[87]

Beyond the fundamental differences at hand, Otis felt insulted that anyone would describe one of his literary efforts as "rash and hasty." He took to the floor of the House and excoriated Parliament. He considered the body no more than a "parcel of Button-makers, Pin-makers, Horse Jockeys, Gamesters, Pensioners, Pimps, and Whore Masters."[88] Bernard thought the performance "the most violent, insolent, abusive, treasonable declamation that perhaps was ever delivered."[89] The General Court then voted on the question to rescind or not. The vote was not close. Ninety-two representatives voted not to rescind, while a mere seventeen wanted to rescind. An angry governor dissolved the legislature, and Boston became more unruly. The government in London responded by sending British Regulars to the town. The 14th and 29th Regiments, along with an artillery company with five fieldpieces, arrived on October 1.

The troops found quarters at Castle William and in public buildings. Their mere presence in the relatively small and compact community irritated the townspeople. Quartering became a major sore point. Otis summarized feelings when the Superior Court convened at the Town House in November. A squad stood guard in the street outside, and other soldiers took up positions in the chamber. As the session opened, Otis jumped to his feet and moved for adjournment to Faneuil Hall since "the stench occasioned by the troops in the representative's' chamber might prove infectious; and that it was utterly derogatory to the court to administer justice at the points of bayonets and the mouths of cannon."[90] Otis continued to protest along these lines for months. Some observers conclude that the war actually began at this time, when the Redcoats first arrived in Boston.

Early in 1769, Bernard instructed Hutchinson to gather evidence on Otis and Samuel Adams in anticipation of the pair going on trial in England for treason. Otis, for his part, began to show signs of tiring. His active law practice, role as leader of the popular party and duties as town moderator became intensely demanding. Increasingly, his emotional and unsteady nature seemed to dominate. During the middle of a legislative session, Otis interrupted the proceedings and blurted out, "Oh Mr. Speaker, the liberty of this country is gone forever! And I'll go after it."[91]

At this time, the board of commissioners of customs, charged with the enforcement of the Navigation Acts regulating American trade, became a focal point of local discontent. A series of newspaper articles signed by "Candidus" attacked the board. There is ample indication that Candidus was Otis. At any rate, Candidus focused on the shortcomings of two commissioners—Paxton and especially John Robinson. "'I must take the liberty to say,' Candidus concluded, 'that had his Majesty's dominions been searched to find out men more thoroughly disgusting to his American subjects (from the knowledge they have of their venal conduct) they could not have been found but in those very persons.'"[92]

Otis showed signs of becoming increasingly concerned that British officials in Boston were laying the groundwork for a formal charge of treason against him. He suspected that Robinson was one of the complainants. Otis sent a letter to the *Boston Gazette* declaring, "Tis strange that Mr. Robinson, even in his Welch clerkship, could not find out that if he '*officially*' or in any other way misrepresents me, I have a natural right if I can get no other satisfaction to break his head."[93]

On September 1, Otis and Samuel Adams met with commissioners Henry Hulton and Robinson. Otis demanded to know if Robinson had ever reported him to be a "rebel and traitor." The commissioner denied doing so, and the men parted in good humor. Two days later, Robinson was surprised to read a letter in the *Gazette* wherein Otis continued to assert, "I have a natural right if I can get no other satisfaction to break his head."[94]

During the evening of the fourth, Otis went to the British Coffee House, a hangout for military and revenue officers. Robinson sat among the patrons. The two exchanged words before Robinson sought to chastise Otis by twisting his nose. In an instant, army and navy officers formed a ring around the two antagonists. The pair went at it, initially with sticks and then with their fists. Otis received the worst of the scrap, suffering a nasty head wound.

Within days, a grand jury found that Robinson had disturbed the peace and "did abuse beat wound and maim" Otis.[95] The court ordered Robinson's appearance on October 31. He posted bond on the twenty-third. He did not appear on the thirty-first, instead sending his attorney. But the court declined to admit the appearance and forfeited his recognizance. At this point, the criminal case disappears from the records, but in January 1770, Otis filed a civil action against his assailant. In March, Robinson pulled up stakes and left for England.

At the same time, bigger events began to dominate the situation. A customs informer in February fired at a gathering and killed a boy. In less than two weeks, a more powerful incident took control. On March 5, elements of 29th Regiment fired on a crowd in front of the Town House and killed five civilians. The infamous Boston Massacre became a major cause célèbre.

The civil case against Robinson came to trial in mid-1771. The jury did "find that the Deft. Is Guilty and also find for the Plant. L2,000 sterling damages and costs."[96] Robinson's attorney entered an appeal. Eventually, in August 1772, when neither party appeared, the court dismissed the case. In the meantime, Otis accepted Robinson's apology and made it clear that it was against his character to seek a monetary settlement for a personal affront. Robinson wound up paying court costs, attorneys' fees and medical costs. In the end, the incident is remarkable because it marked the beginning of a sharp decline in Otis's health and the end of his public service. Admirers felt that the debilitating mental problems that followed traced to Robinson's blow to Otis's head. Be that as it may, as the move for American independence gained momentum, a key player left the stage.

For a period, Otis resumed his law practice, but his health continued to decline. He began to drink heavily and sensed that he had a short time to live. He rued the day he was born and seemed to look forward to the end. On one occasion, he expressed the hope that a bolt of lightning would strike him dead. From time to time, he seemed his old self and spent days at the West Barnstable homestead. In 1775, his sister Mercy Warren cared for him in her Watertown home. Catherine Drinker Bowen, a first-rate biographer and historian, reported that Otis made his way to the June 1775 Battle of Bunker Hill. "Quite insane now, he had somehow wandered off from his sister's house...followed the troops with a borrowed musket and was seen crouching in the trenches, his eye along the gun barrel. At midnight he had

James Otis Jr. grave along the Freedom Trail in downtown Boston. *Courtesy of John Burke.*

stumbled through his sister's door weary and faint. When John [Adams] heard it the tears sprang to his eyes."[97]

In time, he moved to a home in Andover, Massachusetts. In May 1783, the *Boston Gazette* reported, [L]ast Friday Evening, the House of Mr. Isaac Osgood was set on Fire and much shattered by Lightning, by which the Hon. JAMES OTIS, Esq., of this Town, leaning upon this Cane at the front Door, was instantly killed." He "expired without a Groan."[98]

Otis is interred in the Granary Burying Ground on Tremont Street along the Freedom Trail in downtown Boston. While scholars are well aware that Otis acted as one of the foremost intellectual leaders of the movement that led to American independence, a man well known throughout the colonies and in Great Britain, his untimely removal from the scene relegated him to a less eminent status among the American people over following generations. He did not sign famous founding documents, although his words and thoughts run throughout. But he did find his name on the shortlist of those men whom Loyalist officials wanted to send to London to go on trial for treason. In the end, others, including his sister Mercy Otis Warren, took up his cause.

In 1818, Otis's longtime friend John Adams summarized his life better than anyone. "I have been young," said Adams, "and now am old, and

I solemnly say, I have never known a man whose love of his country was more ardent or sincere; never one, who suffered so much; never one, whose services for any ten years of his life were so important and essential to the cause of his country, as those of Mr. Otis from 1760 to 1770."[99]

CHAPTER 6

Mercy Otis Warren

Activist Author

O
f the quartet of illustrious people born in the little village of West Barnstable over a span of several decades in the eighteenth century, Mercy Otis Warren is the least well-known despite a flurry of attention and a number of books in recent years. As early as 1899, this slight received local recognition. The *Patriot* newspaper lamented the fact that the West Barnstable grammar school overlooked the native daughter in an exercise at the end of the academic year. Her brother James, Chief Justice Shaw, Captain Percival, Governor Thomas Hinckley, Reverend Russell and Reverend Enoch Pratt were "the great men and useful men" who were remembered. "It is rather surprising that none of the young ladies" recognized and honored Mercy, a woman who "should not be forgotten in the place of her birth."[100]

The standard history of the town, Donald Trayser's *Barnstable*, accords Mercy no more than a brief mention in passing but devotes an entire part to "some" men of the place (including James Otis Jr., Percival and Shaw). Trayser also gives fair attention to Mercy's young brother Samuel Allyne Otis. While Samuel merits more than passing recognition, he nonetheless did not outshine his older sister. Born at the homestead in 1740, Samuel may be best known for fathering the last great Federalist: Harrison Gray Otis. A Harvard graduate like his father, Samuel served as Speaker of the Massachusetts House of Representatives. A successful merchant, he made an ideal quartermaster of the Continental army. After two years in the Continental Congress, with a push from his ally,

Bas-relief of Otis family by Lloyd Lillie. *Left to right*: James Sr., Samuel, Mercy Warren and James Jr. *Courtesy of Barnstable County-Cataldo Archives.*

vice president–elect John Adams, Samuel became the first secretary of the United States Senate. He is prominently featured in historic illustrations holding the Bible as George Washington took his first oath of office for the presidency. In most settings other than West Barnstable, Samuel Otis would receive much more notice.

In perhaps a greater slight to Mercy, the National Women's Hall of Fame, founded in 1969, did not induct Warren until 2002, intentionally passing over her the year before. And when nominated in 2000, the nomination did not come from an organized group such as a women's organization or historical society. Instead, an individual, unaffiliated man independently submitted her name for consideration. In her day, however, she received much more acclaim.

Born at the homestead on September 25, 1728, Mercy Otis entered a world that generally expected and encouraged little from girls. Domestic household chores formed the limits of a young woman's prospects. Mercy, however, found herself in a fortunate place. Her father, Colonel James, enjoyed stature and financial success. More important, he valued formal education, especially since in his youth he could not take advantage of advanced instruction. Thus, he pushed his children to achieve scholastically.

In this undertaking, the Colonel possessed a valuable ally. His sister Mercy (aunt to young Mercy) married Reverend Johnathan Russell Jr. Russell served as the foremost private tutor in the village. When Russell instructed James Jr. and his brother, sister Mercy usually tagged along. Subjects included English, Greek and Roman literature, the natural sciences and ancient and modern history. She and her siblings were children of the Age of Enlightenment and, therefore, were influenced by the writings and thinking of Sir Isaac Newton and John Locke. Popular literary figures such as Shakespeare and Alexander Pope dominated their studies. Sir Walter Raleigh's *History of the World* gained her favor, and politics in general became preferred material for thought. At an early point, her brother James encouraged her to pursue poetry, a subject close to his heart. All of this was unusual for a girl of the period, but the Otis family, as can be seen, was unusual.

This upbringing helps to explain why Mercy throughout her life remained close to her father and older brother but somewhat distant from her mother. At the height of his career in April 1766, James assured his sister, "This you may depend on, no man ever loved a sister better, and among all my conflicts I never forgot that I am endeavoring to serve you and yours."[101] For her part, five years later, a concerned Mercy told her brother that he was "the continual subject both of my sleeping and waking thoughts."[102]

Perhaps her first trip away from the Cape came in 1743, when she traveled with her father to attend her brother's graduation from Harvard. The celebratory, if not raucous, nature of the event contrasted with her staid, almost Puritanical home life. Mercy experienced her initial view of the outer world when almost fifteen. Tradition indicates that she first met her future husband, James Warren, at the commencement, making it a memorable occasion all round. Young Warren, two years behind James in school, was a close friend of her brother. Tradition overlooks the fact that the elder Warren and Colonel Otis had business dealings as early as the 1730s; thus the families were not strangers at the time of the Harvard ceremony. Eleven years would pass before Mercy and James Warren married. At any rate, father, brother and future husband—the three men most important and influential to her as a young woman—surrounded her during the Harvard visit.

Little is known of Mercy's life in the period between her brother's college graduation and her marriage to James Warren in 1754. One can assume that she continued intellectual pursuits. When she married at the relatively old age of twenty-six, she verged on being considered an "old maid." The wedding united two of the prominent families in the province. The elder Warren accrued wealth as a merchant engaged in coasting and overseas trade. He served as high sheriff of Plymouth County, representative to the General Court and captain in the militia. He died in 1757, leaving his extensive Clifford Farm estate along the Eel River to his son James. Mercy gave birth to their first child, James Jr., in the same year.

Soon the couple moved to town at North and Main Streets. Son Winslow was born in 1759, followed by Charles in 1762, Henry in 1764 and George in 1766. While keenly interested in agriculture and responsible for the farm outside town, James Warren spent most of his time directing the successful business ventures of the family. Also, he received a gubernatorial appointment to succeed his late father as county sheriff. Despite a house full of boys, the relative wealth of the couple enabled Mercy to continue her thoughtful expression and quest for knowledge. In this regard, husband James remained unusually supportive. Their marriage proved strong. Whenever separated, Mercy always in some manner would describe him in her letters as the "affectionate friend of my heart."[103] James would respond in kind.

The record indicates that Mercy did not begin down her literary path until 1766, the year of the birth of her last child. She thereafter set poems to paper from time to time and almost certainly corresponded by letter, although her earliest known letter is one she sent to her brother in 1769. Less than a week after her brother received the grievous head wound in the confrontation with Commissioner John Robinson, she wrote, "You know not what I have suffered for you within the last twenty four hours—I saw you fallen—slain by the hands of merciless men.—I saw your wife a widow, your children orphans, your friends weeping round you, and your country in tears for the man who had sacrificed interest, health, and peace, for the public weal,—but my distress was this evening alleviated by hearing that your life is now not despaired of." Mercy closed, "You will excuse the freedom of my pen, when you consider it held by one who has your welfare more at heart, after a very few exceptions, than that of any other person in the world."[104]

This week in September 1769 turned out to be significant for both brother and sister. James Otis's health, especially his mental health, began to spiral downward. Within two years, a probate court ruled him *non compos mentis* and placed him under the guardianship of brother Samuel. On the other hand, sister Mercy's remarkable literary career took flight. Historians and biographers often suggest that Mercy took up the pen to advance her fading brother's cause.

Early the following year, the Boston Massacre aggravated the discord between the mother country and its American subjects. A meeting at the Warren home, with Samuel Adams in attendance, started the influential

Committees of Correspondence. At this point, Mercy began an important friendship with John and Abigail Adams. Abigail appreciated the advice and thoughts of Mercy, sixteen years her senior. And John engaged in regular political exchanges with Mrs. Warren. In this atmosphere in 1772, Mercy published the first of three bitingly critical plays. *The Adulateur* appeared in the *Massachusetts Spy* newspaper in March and April 1772. In the satire, she engaged the longtime family foe Governor Thomas Hutchinson and ridiculed his hypocrisies of pretending to side with the colonists while working against their interests. Although no cast ever acted the play (Puritanical Boston frowned on such things), printed as a pamphlet, it was widely read by an approving audience, and it remains in print.

A year later, her second play, entitled *The Defeat*, established Mercy as a capable propagandist as well as playwright. The first part appeared in the *Boston Gazette* in May, and the second came in July. Again, Hutchinson served as the villain. In between the two printings, a series of earlier letters written by Hutchinson and Lieutenant Governor Andrew Oliver to Crown officials in London came to light. The correspondence demonstrated Hutchinson's double dealing, and Warren's timely sketch highlighted the fact and presented the man as a traitorous adversary.

Boston appeared to become more unruly by the day. The notorious Tea Party of December 1773 gained the attention of Great Britain. General Thomas Gage replaced Hutchinson as governor, and Parliament passed a number of restrictive laws—the Intolerable Acts, as they became known. The most despised act—the Massachusetts Government Act—abrogated the charter of the Massachusetts Bay Province and gave Gage broad powers. Warren responded with *The Group*, the only play she acknowledged as her writing. In this satire, generally considered the best of the three, Warren offered a clever defense of the developing Patriot cause while reproving American-born Loyalists. As usual, James Warren encouraged his wife's effort, while John Adams offered valued criticism.

A 1776 play called *The Blockheads or The Affrighted Officer*, which defamed British officers, is sometimes attributed to Warren. Published anonymously, the coarse language of the play leads many to discount her authorship. *The Motley Assembly*, a farce, appeared in 1779. Written anonymously, it merits mention only because it is at times credited to Mercy. The latter two plays, regardless of authorship, never gained the importance and influence of Warren's known trio of 1772–75 plays.

During the unrest in Boston leading up to the outbreak of armed hostilities, Mercy did not neglect her strength—poetry. In 1774, she wrote two poems of note. The first, "The Squabble of the Sea Nymphs," celebrated the consequential protest known as the Boston Tea Party. The second poem, "To the Hon. J. Winthrop, Esq.," censured American women who preferred the latest British niceties instead of freedom.

War seemed inevitable in early 1775. With her husband away as a member of the Provincial Congress, Mercy experienced spells of despondency. In a January letter to John Adams, she shared her apprehensions: "You cannot wonder that the timidity, and tenderness of a *woman*, should lead her to wish for a speedy termination of those contests, which interrupt almost every social enjoyment of life, and threaten to spread ruin and devastation over the fairest possessions."[105] James reported from Concord that military supplies were appearing ahead of inhabitants fleeing Boston. He thought that she should prepare to move away from Plymouth and the threat of the British navy. "God has given you great abilities; you have improved them in great Acquirements... They are all now to be called into action for the good of mankind."[106]

The April fights at Lexington and Concord prompted Mercy to hasten preparations to vacate Plymouth for the relative safety of inland Taunton. James made his way to Watertown, the new seat for the Provincial Congress. In June, his cousin Dr. Joseph Warren fell at the Battle of Bunker Hill and James succeeded him as president of the Congress. Within two weeks, he led the delegation welcoming General George Washington, head of the American army, to Cambridge. Mercy busied herself with poetry and letter writing. Her correspondents included John and Abigail Adams, Samuel Adams, Washington, Thomas Jefferson and Alexander Hamilton. Perhaps her most important correspondent turned out to be Catharine Macaulay, a British historian familiar to the Washingtons and other American revolutionaries. The pair discussed politics and feminist issues. Macaulay influenced Warren's writing especially as it related to her largest production, an upcoming history of the war for independence.

Mercy came up with the idea of writing a book on the history of the Revolution at about the time open combat commenced. Through her husband especially, she had ready access and frequent exposure to many of the key American players in the unfolding drama. She set down an introductory outline and began to amass notes. While much of the news in the winter of 1775–76 proved discouraging, in March the British felt it advisable to evacuate their forces from besieged Boston. The town returned to Patriot hands. Several months later, a large crowd gathered below the Town House balcony to hear independence proclaimed. Bells rang and cannons roared.

The theater of war moved southward, and in the months to follow, the political influence of the Warrens declined. In 1778, Massachusetts voters rejected a state constitution that James Warren played a significant part in preparing. More hurtful, his district declined to send him back to the legislature. For his part, James walked away from appointments to key governmental posts. Meanwhile, the couple found a new object of scorn. John Hancock, playing politics down the middle, continued to amass a fortune and vie for political advancement. Mercy saw a shift away from virtue and the original revolutionary objectives and decried the increasing worship of wealth. She published a poem entitled "Genius of America" to make her point. Ending the year on a melancholy note, in November, Colonel Otis, the patriarch of the family, passed away at the family homestead in West Barnstable.

As the war wound down, the Warrens moved to Milton, Massachusetts, in early June 1781, purchasing the former home of no less than the disdained Thomas Hutchinson. They made their move just in time to receive their eldest son, Lieutenant James Jr., home from the sea. Serving under legendary Captain John Barry on the American frigate *Alliance*, thirty-six guns, young Warren suffered a serious leg wound in a May 29 sea fight off Cape Sable, Nova Scotia. In the action, the *Alliance* took the British sloop of war *Atalanta*, sixteen guns, and brig sloop *Trepassy*, fourteen guns, and limped back to Boston. After a few days of suffering at the new family home, young James agreed to have his leg amputated. The news got worse. Several years later, son Charles died among strangers in distant St. Lucar, Spain.

The months passed, and Mercy continued to write poems and plays while paying close attention to politics and the new government. In 1786, the infamous Shays' Rebellion in western Massachusetts made it clear that the governing Articles of Confederation presented problems for the new country. As a result, a national constitutional convention convened in Philadelphia in mid-1787. This set the stage for Mercy to take a role in the great public debate that followed. By this time, the Warrens were Anti-Federalists, or the faction interested in retaining existing local power and influence and avoiding central tyranny. The opposition Federalists, on the other hand, pushed for a strong general government to avoid chaos such as the Shays affair. John Adams differed with the Warrens and favored the latter system. This as much as anything explains why the once close Adams-Warren relationship cooled.

As soon as the convention presented its proposed constitution, Massachusetts questioned the document. Mercy became one of the ardent critics. She set about writing a nineteen-page pamphlet, *Observations on the New Constitution, and on the Federal and State Conventions, by a Columbian Patriot.* For a great while, observers incorrectly attributed the piece to Elbridge Gerry, a Massachusetts delegate. Gerry, in fact, offered his own critique at the time in the form of a paper titled "Hon. Mr. Gerry's Objections." Other leading lights such as Patrick Henry and Samuel Adams took similar stands. Among Mercy's criticisms, the draft constitution did not contain a bill of rights; it accorded the president princely powers; it did not deal with executive and judicial branch overlapping; and it presented the threat of a standing army.

A rowdy Massachusetts state convention convened in January 1788. Although the Anti-Federalists sent more delegates, the Federalists demonstrated greater skill and enthusiasm. After considerable politicking and a fistfight between Gerry and Federalist Francis Dana, and before Mercy's critique made it to print, the convention ratified the proposed constitution while offering a few amendments. The Warrens did not think the amendments went far enough. Virginia and New York followed the Massachusetts lead and suggested their own amendments.

When the First Congress convened, James Madison wanted to avoid and preempt a second national constitutional convention, so he offered ten congressional amendments. The changes became known as the Bill of Rights. All of this provided Mercy and the other critics some satisfaction. But the stress was enough to prompt the Warrens to give up on their Milton residence and return to familiar Plymouth.

Poorly informed modern admirers of Mercy Otis Warren often exaggerate her part in the foregoing debate. Some incorrectly credit her with a central if not primary role in producing the Bill of Rights. In the end, her voice was one of many. What made her unique—and her contribution unique—was the fact she was a woman skillfully operating in a domain reserved for men.

In 1790, Mercy published a volume of her poems under the title of *Poems, Dramatic and Miscellaneous.* President Washington gave his permission for her dedication to him, saying that he was "duly sensible of the Merits of the respectable and amiable writer."[107] She sent complimentary copies to notables such as Washington, Gerry, John Adams, Henry Knox and Alexander Hamilton. With this book, along with Anne Bradstreet and Phillis Wheatley, Mercy became one of the first female poets to publish in her own name in America. But her magnum opus remained in the future.

Within months, heartache paid another visit. Winslow, Mercy's favorite son and frequent disappointment, received a second lieutenant's commission in

Statue of Mercy Otis Warren on the lawn of the Superior Courthouse, Barnstable. *Courtesy of John Burke.*

the army. In a few weeks, he found himself in the wilderness of the Northwest Territory, serving under General Arthur St. Clair. In mid-December, the awful news reached Massachusetts. On November 4, 1791, a confederation of Indian tribes had trapped St. Clair's one-thousand-man unit on a little hill along the Wabash River and wiped out the force. Only forty-eight soldiers escaped. Winslow did not make it out. Upon hearing the report, young Harrison Gray Otis responded as one who was intimately familiar with Winslow's mother. "'Good God,' he cried, 'what a dismal Stroke for poor Aunt Warren, it will kill her I fear.'"[108]

Mercy retreated to her desk and writing, always a comfort. Her book needed renewed attention. Despite repeated personal setbacks and other discouragements, she persisted toward her goal. Macaulay's earlier visit in 1784 provided lasting motivation. Along the way, old friend John Adams stepped in and encouraged her project. "I hope you will continue [it], for there are few Persons possessed of more Facts, or who can record them in a more agreeable manner."[109] She maintained a brisk correspondence with friends such as Gerry, Henry Knox and Benjamin Lincoln, seeking background information and piling up notes. Winslow's death would be a lasting wound. However, Mercy recalled, he had encouraged and promoted her book project more than others. "'Revise & correct and make it perfect,' he had said, 'for which you ought to appropriate a number of hours every day.'"[110]

The divisiveness in the country in the last decade of the eighteenth century discouraged Mercy. An unhappy ending to the great experiment would not be a fitting conclusion to her history. Then, as the new century began, unthinkable news arrived from Maine. After an illness of more than a month, son George passed away. Once again, Mercy handled grief by concentrating on her writing. By this time, her eyesight had begun to fail. Son James Jr., still in the house, helped her address the handicap. Dr. James Freeman, minister of King's Chapel in Boston, provided considerable editorial assistance and guidance, acting in the ways of a modern agent. In addition, he proved effective as a solicitor of subscriptions.

The fact that so many histories on the Revolution began to appear gave greater urgency to her task. The history authored by John Marshall offered stiff competition. Warren thought that she could separate from the pack by putting forward the truth in an objective manner. But she found it difficult to maintain impartiality. Her tone became Republican, and her sketches of the key actors proved plainspoken. Friend John Adams presented a bewildering hurdle. Hands down an early Patriot, his public conduct now demonstrated a predilection for monarchy. Her treatment of Adams led to a further cooling of their relationship, although in her final years, the two restored their valued friendship.

Finally, in 1805, the first volume of *History of the Rise, Progress, and Termination of the American Revolution, Interspersed with Biographical, Political, and Moral Observations* appeared. Mercy decided on the title early in the project. The third and final volume came out in 1806. A mixed reception followed. Jefferson, of a similar political bent, liked the work and purchased copies for his close circle. Federalists, however, did not appreciate her political

The Paul Revere bell, donated to the West Parish meetinghouse by Colonel James Otis. *Private collection.*

tone. In the end, the work proved to be about Warren as much as about the Revolution.

The years following were not golden for Mercy. James died in 1808, not fully appreciated as an early and devoted Patriot and public servant. A Jefferson supporter, she lived in a region adamantly opposed to the president's embargo, adopted in 1807. Moreover, her son Henry served as the collector of the Plymouth port, and her brother Joseph acted in the same capacity at Barnstable. They were charged with enforcing the hated law. As troublesome, her nephew Harrison Gray Otis became a leading opponent of the Jefferson and Madison administrations and their embargo and war policies. In fact, more than anyone, he acted as the primary force behind the infamous Hartford Convention. Mercy, however, did not have to bear witness to the meeting itself. She died on October 19, 1814, days before the gathering convened in Connecticut. She outlived her parents, of course, her husband, all her siblings and three of her five children. Mercy rests at Burial Hill in Plymouth.

For years, the Paul Revere bell donated to the West Barnstable meetinghouse by Colonel Otis served as the only visible (and audible) reminder of the Otis family in the village. The homestead decayed, and later occupants removed the remains by the 1830s. Heirs retained the property until the mid-nineteenth century. In 1855, the remaining forty-four acres went on the market. The house itself occupied a spot across the highway from the existing Cooperative Bank and close to the ancient Hinckley's Lane and Proctor's railroad crossing. In 1917, the Sons of the Revolution placed a boulder with a bronze plaque along the nearby roadway to memorialize James Otis Jr.

In 1991, a collection of citizens led by Louis Cataldo of Barnstable erected a James Otis Jr. memorial statue on the lawn of the Barnstable Superior Courthouse. Ten years later, the same group placed a companion statue of Mercy Otis Warren close by. Local sculptor David Lewis created both pieces. In a related undertaking, since 2002, several organizations have banded together to bestow a Mercy Otis Warren Cape Cod Woman of the Year award on an outstanding woman of the county. Much earlier, in 1785, John Adams expressed the sense of those behind the foregoing efforts. One of his letters to Thomas Jefferson reads, in part, "I declare, I don't believe there is one family upon Earth to which the United States are so much indebted for their Preservation from Thralldom. There was scarcely any Family in New England had such Prospects of Opulence and Power under Royal Government. They have sacrificed all."[111]

CHAPTER 7

Mad Jack Percival

Naval Legend

John Percival Jr. remained connected to and fond of his hometown to a greater degree than many people who travel and earn an international reputation. An incident from one of his later cruises demonstrates. A seaman returned from shore drunk. Percival ordered the mate to seize the malefactor, bare his back and bind him by the wrists to the shrouds. Directed to administer ten lashes as punishment, another mate approached with the dreaded cat-o-nine-tails. The seaman turned to Mad Jack and pleaded, "Captain, spare me. I'm from your hometown Barnstable."

"You rascal, you'll get five more for disgracing the place!" roared Percival.

The typical story leads some to assume that Percival behaved as a tyrant, especially with such a threatening nickname. The facts show otherwise. Although a firm disciplinarian, he was fair. His crews and young officers adored him. Percival's origins and early experience help explain.

Born on April 3, 1779, in the family home on Scorton Hill in West Barnstable, John Jr. was one of five children of John Percival Sr. and Mary Snow Percival. Both the senior Percival and his wife came from families who knew their way around the water. Mary Snow's father worked as a sea captain. Her oldest child, Abigail, married John Crocker Jr., another sailing captain. And Mad Jack's younger brother Isaac spent his life on the sea, rising to master. As significant, the elder Percival spent considerable time in the merchant service. The experience served him well, earning him command of the privateer galley *Anti Smuggler*.

Owned by Nathaniel Freeman and others of Sandwich, Massachusetts, the *Anti Smuggler* received its privateering commission in August 1782, little more than a year before the end of the Revolutionary War. Percival and two Boston associates put up a $20,000 bond and enlisted an eighteen-man crew. The vessel, like so many privateers of the period, did not appear imposing. It carried only small arms. Nonetheless, in December, it made five captures, including the one-hundred-ton brigantine *Nancy*, the one-hundred-ton schooner *Sally* and the thirty-ton schooner *Dolly*, as well as a pair of two-masted, six-ton boats. How much profit Percival realized is not clear. But one thing is certain: the adventurous father impressed his young son.

As much as people from any other place, the men of Cape Cod at this time tied themselves to the sea. Relatively poor soil barred all but subsistence farming. The oceans became their gardens. Numerous excellent harbors encouraged maritime pursuits. By the Federalist period (1765–1815), the New England region had developed a single-minded attachment to waterborne commerce. Under these conditions, it became natural for young Percival to turn to the sea.

There are not too many historic personalities who are featured in more tall tales than John Percival. The myths and the legend began when he left home for the sea at age thirteen. As the story goes, Percival became displeased with the food at home and decided to leave. He did not have a destination, so he stood on a boulder along the marsh shore and spun around and around until dizziness caused him to fall to the ground. He determined to strike out in the direction he faced as he got to his feet. As luck would have it, he looked to the northwest and Boston. The fanciful tale overlooks the fact that at thirteen Percival was older than many of the countless Cape Cod boys who naturally elected seafaring. The historian John Palfrey made the point, noting, "The duck does not take to the water with a surer instinct than the Barnstable boy," who "can hand, reef, and steer, by the time he flies a kite."[112]

Percival began as most youngsters did, as a cabin boy and cook on a coaster. Within four years, he had risen to second mate in the merchant service. A year later, he went out on the *Thetis* under Captain David Crocker. The ship made a stop at Dunkirk and moved down to Lisbon in February 1797, an unsuitable time to be in the area. British admiral Sir John Jervis had just defeated a Spanish fleet off Portugal's Cape Saint Vincent. The British had 73 men killed and 327 wounded. Moreover, four Spanish prizes required crews. The Royal Navy sent a request to shore for replacements, and a Portuguese press gang went into action. On February 24, Percival fell victim to its sweep. Upon being impressed, the British received Percival on Jervis's flagship, the HMS *Victory*, one hundred guns, Captain Robert Calder commanding.

Within a few weeks, the Brits transferred Percival to an eighteen-gun brig. While on patrol, the brig narrowly escaped capture by a Spanish sail of the line. Seeking cover in the Canary Islands, the British vessel managed to capture a Spanish merchantman. The brig's skipper designated Percival a member of the prize crew under command of the brig's doctor. The captured vessel sailed for Madeira. Upon arrival, Percival learned that the captain of the American ship *Washington*, in port, needed more crewmen. Lax discipline prevailed on the prize, and Percival managed to overpower the officer of the deck. His cohorts quickly bound and gagged the frightened officer. The band took one of the vessel's boats and rowed out of the harbor to meet the waiting *Washington*.

But Percival remained in danger. Bound eventually for Boston, the *Washington* encountered problems off Java. The Dutch navy impressed Percival and put him on its frigate *Samarang*. In short order, he managed to escape again and found his way to England on the East India Company's ship *Rose*. There he found work on the American merchantman *Hector* and made his way back to the United States.

His brief tenure on the fabled *Victory* resulted in another persistent yarn. The story, without foundation, places Mad Jack in command of the foretop of the *Victory* during Lord Nelson's famous 1805 Battle of Trafalgar. The origin of the story remains unknown. Percival never told it. For his part, Percival acknowledged that he resided in a Santa Cruz, Tenerife prison at about the time of the memorable sea fight. Officials there deprived him of his ship and threw him in the city jail. A British merchant captain helped him escape and carried him to London. Percival thereupon made his way back home.

Already a veteran of brief service in the British and Dutch navies, in 1798 Percival decided to try his hand with the U.S. Navy. In April, Congress established the Department of the Navy as Franco-American relations deteriorated. Three months later, President John Adams authorized American navy ships to seize French vessels, beginning the brief Quasi-War with France. In July, Percival signed on as a master's mate with the USS *Delaware*, twenty guns, Captain Thomas Baker commanding.

The *Delaware* cruised in the West Indies and, in early October, helped the USS *Pickering*, fourteen guns, make two captures. Late in the month, on its own, Baker's ship captured the French privateer brig *Ocean*. In November, Baker put in at Curacao in the Netherlands Antilles, remaining there for weeks due to sickness on board. In May, the navy ordered the ship to return to New Castle. A second message from the department announced Percival's promotion to midshipman, effective May 13, 1800. Baker turned his ship over to Captain J.A. Spotswood. Percival remained in place for an uneventful year.

In July 1801, hostilities ceased, and the navy downsized. Anticipating peace, Congress in March enacted legislation to reduce the naval officer corps by three-fifths. Twenty ships and their crews were released, while the service retained fourteen ships with their crews. Originally the merchantman *Hamburg Packet*, officials judged the *Delaware* too slow. The service decommissioned it and released Percival and the entire crew. The judgments on the ships seemed sound, but the manner of separating personnel proved arbitrary. Many good men received discharges, and many poor performers remained. Percival spent the next eight years in the merchant marine, most of it in European and West Indies waters.

Within a year of his naval release, Percival stumbled on personal tragedy in France. Arriving in Bordeaux, he spotted a familiar but forlorn face. His father was wandering the docks. The British seized the elder Percival's vessel and refused to compensate him. Destitute, he made his way across the English Channel from London, hoping to find a way home. Percival carried his sick sixty-two-year-old father to his ship and headed for America. Tragically, John Sr. died en route, compelling his son to bury him at sea. A stone in the West Barnstable cemetery solemnizes this unhappy outcome.

The first decade of the 1800s turned out to be a dismal time for New England shipping interests. Jefferson, concerned about repeated British interference with American vessels and impressment of American seamen, initiated an embargo in 1807. The measure kept United States vessels in port and out of harm's way. The tactic had the effect of decimating the country's merchant marine and fishing fleets. Sections of the coastline found half the men unemployed. Banks failed, and poorhouses turned needy away. Rhode Island, as one example, experienced an 85 percent drop in exports in 1808.

Percival's hometown found itself among the few places in the region that supported Jefferson. Moreover, Percival held a personal grudge in the developing squabble. Quite familiar with the outrageous Royal Navy practice of impressment, he also attributed his father's untimely death to British highhandedness. Percival contacted his former skipper, Captain Baker, and requested a recommendation for naval service. Baker complied, and on March 6, 1809, the West Barnstable native returned to the U.S. Navy. He received an appointment as sailing master assigned to Virginia's Norfolk Navy Yard.

The navy placed him on the USS *Syren*, sixteen guns, where he served an uneventful term ending in November.

During his *Syren* service, Percival achieved a personal milestone. On September 27, 1809, he married Maria Pinkerton in Norfolk County, Virginia, now the city of Chesapeake. There is an untold story behind the wedding. The bride was a daughter of Dr. David Smith and Mary Fitzrandolph Pinkerton of Trenton, New Jersey. James Smith made oath that Maria was of lawful age. She had turned sixteen a month earlier. Percival was thirty. The question persists: how did a refined teenager wind up married to an older, rough-and-tumble mariner? Although childless, the couple remained close to the end of their days.

The crisis with the British seemed to subside toward the end of the year, and in December, the navy placed Percival and many others on extended furlough. Things took a bellicose turn, and in June 1812, the United States declared war against Great Britain. In August, Percival returned to duty at the New York Navy Yard. Officials placed him in command of U.S. gunboat No. 6. Boats of this type were designed for port defense. They carried a medium bow gun and a smaller stern gun, as well as a crew of about three dozen.

Percival saw his first gunboat action in early November when the HMS *Plantagenet*, seventy-four guns, Captain R. Lloyd commanding, chased the American schooner *Sparrow* on shore at Long Branch. Percival led gunboats to the rescue. When the Americans arrived, they found the Brits climbing about the grounded schooner. Percival deployed his men and poured a heavy fire at the enemy. "After a very spirited resistance on both sides," Percival reported, "we succeeded in driving them off."[113] When the British boarding party returned to their ship, the *Plantagenet* opened up with its heavy guns, forcing the Yanks to take cover. The British sent their barges back toward the schooner, but Percival's men drove them back. At this point, Lloyd called things off, leaving the shattered *Sparrow* to the Americans. In the months to follow, Mad Jack became involved in a series of similar skirmishes around the entrance to New York.

However, Percival found it unnecessary to rely on gunboats to garner attention. The British sloop *Eagle*, a tender for Admiral J.B. Beresford's flagship HMS *Poictiers*, seventy-four guns, busied itself for weeks plaguing New York coasters and fishermen. U.S. Commodore Jacob Lewis told Percival to address the problem. Percival went down to the Fly Market on the East River and borrowed a fishing smack fittingly named the *Yankee*. He placed various livestock on its deck and gathered thirty-six volunteers. He armed thirty-four and hid them in the cabin and forepeak. The visible calf,

Lieutenant John Percival in about 1817 from a portrait by Ethan A. Greenwood, in the possession of the U.S. Naval Academy. *Courtesy of U.S. Department of the Navy.*

sheep and geese served as bait. Percival and two others donned traditional fisherman's gear. Early on July 4, they "stood out to sea as if going on a fishing voyage to the banks."[114]

The vigilant *Eagle* spotted the fisherman as it passed the Hook and promptly overhauled it. Master's Mate H. Morris admired the livestock and ordered Percival to carry it down to Beresford on his flagship. Percival acknowledged the order and put up the helm, apparently for the purpose. He slipped closer to the *Eagle*, and when within three yards, he shouted, "Lawrence!" Upon hearing the watchword, the armed men rushed on deck and fired into the *Eagle* "a volley of musketry which struck her crew, with dismay, and drove them all down so precipitately into the hold of the vessel, that they had not time to strike their colors."[115]

Percival crossed over to the *Eagle* and tried to comfort the wounded Morris. The Brit raised himself to one elbow and mumbled, "We have had enough of you!"[116] He then fell back and expired. A few hours later, Percival returned with his capture to Whitehall "amidst the shouts and plaudits of thousands of spectators assembled on the Battery, celebrating the Fourth of July."[117] Many years later, the New England folklorist Alton Blackington observed that Percival "knew how to celebrate July 4th without listening to a band concert."[118]

When Master Commandant Lewis Warrington needed a sailing master for his sloop of war USS *Peacock*, twenty-two guns, he knew where to turn. He knew Percival from Norfolk in 1809, but the latter's recent escapades helped decide the selection. In any event, Percival joined the *Peacock* crew at New York early in March 1814 and took the helm a few days later when the ship slipped past the British blockade and headed south. A month later, the Americans spotted a Royal Navy brig escorting three merchant ships off Cape Canaveral, Florida. The enemy warship turned out to be the HMS *Epervier*, twenty guns, Richard Wales commanding, out of Halifax, Nova Scotia, commanding.

After a brief chase, the two ships closed. The *Epervier* fired its starboard guns, and the *Peacock* responded in kind. The British shots went high but managed to strike the Americans' foreyard, depriving Percival of his fore and foretop sails. The damage forced Percival to keep his ship large throughout the rest of the fight. The *Epervier* eased off, assumed a parallel course and found itself in grave trouble. Its carronades were showing defects, unshipping due to defective fighting-bolts. The *Peacock* poured a withering fire into its antagonist, ripping away rigging and spars. Wales found himself unable to maneuver and almost without firepower. He called for boarders, but his men declined. He had no choice but to surrender. The fierce fight lasted nine minutes. Eleven British sailors were killed and fifteen wounded. The Americans suffered but two wounded.

The American press bragged endlessly. The *Connecticut Courant*, for instance, suggested that the *Peacock* had "adorned with another most brilliant laurel, the naval history of our country."[119] In his report to the Navy Department, Warrington declared that Percival had "handled the ship, as if he had been working her into a roadstead."[120] Later, Congress awarded gold and silver medals to the *Peacock* officers and swords to the midshipmen and sailing master.

Shortly thereafter, the *Peacock* sailed on a successful cruise up and down the west coast of Great Britain and down to Cape Verde. During the 147-day run, it took or destroyed fourteen British merchant ships totaling 2,364 tons worth some $610,000. While refitting in New York, Percival received

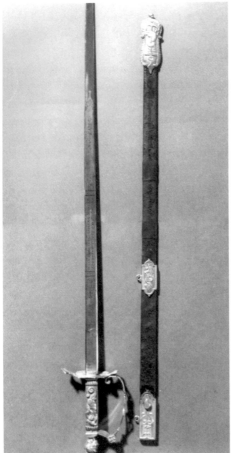

Above: Depiction of the 1814 sea fight between the USS *Peacock* and the HMS *Epervier*. *Private collection.*

Left: Sword awarded by Congress to John Percival for heroism in the War of 1812. *Courtesy of U.S. Naval Academy Museum.*

word that President James Madison had signed his promotion to lieutenant, effective December 9, 1814. By this time, the nickname "Mad Jack" had begun to be applied to the man. Its origin is unclear, but Percival appreciated and encouraged its use.

On January 22, 1815, although peace appeared imminent, three American warships, including the *Peacock*, passed out of New York bound for an extended cruise against the enemy. By May, Warrington had found himself alone in the Indian Ocean, completely unaware that the United States ratified a peace settlement on February 17. On June 30, 1815, flying British colors, the *Peacock* passed up the Sunda Strait and came upon the English East India Company's brig *Nautilus*, sixteen guns, Lieutenant Charles Boyce commanding. Warrington ran up the Stars and Stripes, prompting Boyce to inquire if the Americans knew of the peace. Warrington replied that if peace prevailed, Boyce should haul his colors down as a token. If he did not, Warrington said, he'd fire into the Brit. Boyce refused, and a *Peacock* forward gun discharged. The *Nautilus* promptly retaliated with a broadside. The Americans countered, and the *Nautilus* struck. The skirmish killed six *Nautilus* men and wounded eight others. The Americans escaped unscathed. While the British complained and its press howled, the department absolved Warrington of any wrongdoing.

The engagement became significant because it turned out to be the last combat of the unwanted War of 1812. And it marked the end of a commendable campaign by the *Peacock*. During the war, only twenty-two U.S. Navy ships made it to sea. They took a total of 165 prizes. The *Peacock* by itself took 19 prizes, or 12 percent of the total.

The navy detached Percival from the *Peacock* in March 1816 and assigned him to the Boston Navy Yard and the USS *Macedonian*, thirty-eight guns. This assignment brought him into contact with the yard's commandant, Captain Isaac Hull. The illustrious former commander of "Old Ironsides" and Mad Jack became close, lifelong friends. They held each other in high regard. Hull's esteem for Percival is best illustrated by an incident that took place many years later, in 1839. Hull commanded the Mediterranean squadron at the time and had the swift *Ohio*, sixty-four guns, as his flagship. Percival commanded the *Cyane*, twenty-two guns. Hull ordered his little fleet to sail to a particular harbor. Custom and prudence called for subordinates to follow the flagship into port. But when Hull and the *Ohio* arrived, they found Percival and the *Cyane* at anchor.

When Mad Jack went on the flagship to pay his respects, Hull demanded to know why he had forged ahead. "Give me the 'Ohio' when we go back, and you take the 'Cyane,'" replied Percival, "and I'll get there first!"

Softening, Hull agreed. "I have no doubt you would, for Jack, you are the best sailor I ever saw!"[121]

Another example of Percival's storied seamanship dates to his *Macedonian* days. Captain John Downes took the ship out of Boston in the fall of 1818 and headed for the west coast of South America. It got in trouble near Bermuda, caught up in a tremendous hurricane. For more than fifteen hours, the "indescribably awful" storm battered the ship.[122] Sails parted and split. The mizzenmast sprung in two places and went by the board. The foremast sprung in three or four places, and the main topmast went over the side. What remained of the lower sections of the main and foremasts banged away at the keel. Another officer hurried to Percival and told him that the carpenter was starting to cut away the mainmast. Veteran seaman Percival knew that the mast would be critical to the ship's survival in the hours to come. Mad Jack raced to the scene and bellowed above the raging storm, "Avast there, or we shall all be in eternity in five minutes!"[123] The carpenter dropped his axe, permitting the mast to remain and offer limited use in the hours to come. Percival's official service record credits this quick action with saving the big ship.

In September 1823, the department transferred Percival to the *United States*, fifty-six guns, under Hull. In December, along with the schooner *Dolphin*, twelve guns, the ship sailed for the west coast of South America to protect American business and whaling interests in the region. On January 26, 1824, a terrible mutiny took place on the Nantucket whaler *Globe* in the vicinity of Fanning Island in the South Pacific. Twenty-year-old Samuel Comstock led the mutiny. Comstock and his coconspirators killed the captain and first, second and third mates and took control of the *Globe*. A few weeks later, while the mutineers and other crewmen were on shore at Mili in the Mulgraves, harpooner Gilbert Smith and a few sympathizers managed to escape in the ship. They arrived in Valparaiso, Chile, in June 1824. Word of the crime reached Nantucket in October. Whaling interests on the island immediately petitioned the government in Washington to do something. Late in May 1825, Hull received departmental instructions to do what he could at that late date.

Hull dispatched Percival in the *Dolphin*, ordering him to search for the mutineers and stop off at the Sandwich Islands on his way back. He had little trouble completing his crew. Men from the squadron pleaded to be included. Adventure, of course, acted as an attraction. But something else served as motivation. All of his crews held Percival in great esteem. Over the years, a number of sailors who served with Percival penned glowing sketches of the man. F.P. Torrey's summation is typical. "[H]e is spoken of by his men in high terms of praise; he is said truly to be the seaman's friend, and keeps a bright lookout for their welfare," wrote Torrey. "No better sailor was ever upon salt water than Captain Percival; he has great activity and spirit, is slim built, near six feet in height; he is plain in his dress, frank and open in manners."[124]

In any event, Percival got underway on August 18. While watering the ship north of Western Samoa, the Americans encountered unfriendly and thievish natives. A resolute show of force controlled the situation, and on November 19, the schooner reached the Mulgraves. A search of the many islets proceeded. Before long, the navy men began to find evidence from the *Globe*. On the tenth day of searching, a *Dolphin* boat crew encountered a hostile band of about one hundred natives on a beach. To their surprise, one man stepped forward and shouted, "Don't come on shore unless you are prepared to fight. The islanders are going to kill you."[125] The man turned out to be William Lay, an innocent *Globe* crewman who missed his chance to escape with Smith.

Events moved rapidly at this point. The American search party found a second innocent, Cyrus Hussey. The natives had adopted the two young whalers. Comstock and all of his fellow mutineers were dead, killed by the natives or by one another. Mad Jack took the time to lecture the natives about their proclivities for stealing, lying and general immorality. If they ever killed or injured another white man, he said, the U.S. Navy would return and blot out every soul on the islands and destroy their fruit trees. Having made his point, he changed his tenor and handed out gifts—hatchets, beads and cloth. News of the successful investigation and recovery did not reach Nantucket until August 26, 1826. Historians credit Percival's extraordinary success with the fact that a *Globe*-like mutiny was not repeated in the American-Pacific whale fishery.

But the *Dolphin* was only halfway home. The most colorful and controversial leg of the trip remained. On January 15, 1826, the schooner arrived at Oahu, the first U.S. Navy man-of-war to visit the Sandwich Islands (now Hawaii). The stay proved tumultuous and legendary.

Percival stepped into a major controversy. Reverend Hiram Bingham of the Boston-based American Mission Board had submitted a formal proposal to the local government that would make the Ten Commandments the law of the islands. Regents for the youthful King Kamehameha III favored the plan, while other influential native leaders and foreign merchants opposed the scheme. A leading Hawaiian told Percival that Bingham represented himself as an agent of the American government. Percival also learned that when Lord George Byron visited the place the year before, he felt that Bingham appeared as an inveterate meddler in public affairs. At the outset, Percival went out of his way to treat the missionaries with politeness. He made it clear when his men were on shore on Sundays that they were expected to attend church first and frolic afterward. He gave the missionaries several dozen bottles of wine as a goodwill gesture. But he also engaged Bingham in debate and scoffed at his claim that he represented the United States government. In Percival's mind, he served as the sole representative of the American government, and he displayed little interest in sharing the duty. The stage was set.

The growing controversy assumed a titillating aspect when at the behest of the missionaries, the local authorities banned visits by native women to ships in the harbor. Much back and forth transpired, and the missionaries reported that Mad Jack threatened to blow the town down if the prohibition remained. On Sunday afternoon, February 25, a bored collection of seamen decided to take action. The angry men interrupted a prayer meeting at Prime Minister Kalanimoku's house and demanded women. Failing, the group hurled stones at his windows. Reverend Bingham made a dash for his nearby dwelling, a gang at his heels. When Percival heard of the affray, he raced to the scene along with two midshipmen and several whaling captains. Mad Jack, with his umbrella, leveled the first miscreant he encountered, roaring, "I'll teach you to disgrace us!"[126]

Percival flogged some of the navy participants and confined others. The local authorities assessed the situation, and the governor lifted the ban. They believed that with four to five hundred seamen in port, the law against lewd women seemed unenforceable. In honor of Percival's concern for his men, to this day, United States destroyer squadrons based at Pearl Harbor celebrate Mad Jack Percival Day each May 11, the date the *Dolphin* left the islands in 1826.

But the missionaries complained endlessly to the American government and public. A pair of sea captains whom Percival had crossed sided with the Bingham forces. Consequently, Percival asked for a court of inquiry to clear his name. After hesitating, the secretary convened a court in June 1828. Six months later, the secretary ruled the complaints meritless, but he declared that Percival should have shown more restraint in the presence of impressionable Hawaiians. Otherwise, the secretary commended Percival for his overall performance during the cruise.

After an extended leave, Mad Jack received in August 1830 command of the U.S. schooner *Porpoise*, twelve guns, and sailed against the troublesome

The U.S. schooner *Dolphin*, Lieutenant John Percival commanding, departing Oahu in May 1826. *Courtesy of Raymond A. Massey.*

pirates in the West Indies. A year later, his health began to decline, and he went on another lengthy leave, spending much of his time in West Barnstable. During the period, he received the welcome news that the navy had promoted him to master commandant, retroactive to March 3, 1831. In May 1834, he took command of the sloop of war *Erie*, twenty-two guns, and sailed to the Brazil Station. He left the ship in August 1835 and went on leave. By this point, he had established his home on Meeting House Hill in the Dorchester section of Boston. On July 1, 1836, he reported back for duty at the Charlestown yard, assigned duty as the executive officer.

Just two days earlier, a train of the Boston and Providence Rail Road Corporation had crashed, injuring a score of sailors transferring from Brooklyn to Boston. As executive officer, Percival stepped in to act on their behalf. The otherwise routine affair is not noteworthy except for the fact that in 1993, a biographer completely ignored the record and falsely accused Mad Jack of stealing the $12,862 insurance settlement received by four of the injured men and entrusted to his administration. Percival kept detailed and faithful account of every cent. The men or their heirs received every penny due, and Percival, of course, did not charge for his work. The ponderous and sometimes almost illegible trust records that tell this story were donated to the Massachusetts Historical Society, where they can be viewed. A microfilm of the same records can be found in the archives of Barnstable's Sturgis Library. Nobody believes that the biographer acted out of malice. All of the evidence suggests that he relied on sloppy and insufficient research conducted on his behalf. This issue is worth clarifying because the deficient biography is out there, and although Percival had his faults, improbity was not one of them.

In April 1837, the board of navy commissioners assigned Percival a task right up his alley. A dispute raged over the best location for a lighthouse along Nauset Beach on Cape Cod. He visited Eastham, studied the matter and urged a three-tower plan. He located the spots for each light. The famed Three Sisters lights were completed in 1838 according to his layout.

While busy at the Boston yard in June 1837, he entertained Nathaniel Hawthorne and Maine congressman Jonathan Cilley while aboard the revenue cutter *Hamilton*. Hawthorne wrote a perceptive extended description of Percival. In brief, Hawthorne noted that Mad Jack "seems to have moulded and shaped himself to his own whims, til a sort of rough affectation has become thoroughly imbued throughout a kindly nature…Percival seems to be the very pattern of old integrity; taking as much care of Uncle Sam's interests as if all the money expended were to come out of his own pocket… [A]t any rate, he now passes his life with a sort of gruff contentedness, grumbling and growling, yet in good humor enough."[127]

Other authors of note found Percival good material. Herman Melville, for example, used him as the basis of a favorable character in *White-Jacket*. His fictional Lieutenant Mad Jack is patterned after Percival. The officer and the author were on familiar terms. Percival's lifelong friend Lemuel Shaw, chief justice of the Massachusetts Supreme Judicial Court at the time, was close to the Melville family. A young Shaw was betrothed to Herman's aunt Nancy Melvill, who died soon after the engagement. When he did marry, Shaw had a daughter, Elizabeth. She married Herman Melville. And when Herman spent time away, the Percivals often accompanied Mrs. Melville to the theater in Boston. Melville summarized his Lieutenant Mad Jack, and thus Percival the man, as "a bit of a tyrant—they say all good officers are—but the sailors loved him all round; and would much rather stand fifty watches with him, than one with a rose-water sailor."[128]

In April 1838, the department assigned Percival command of the *Cyane* in the Mediterranean under Hull. Late in 1839, he relinquished the post due to persistent ailments, particularly gout and rheumatism. The cruise, however, demonstrated Percival's deep interest in naval education and the well-being of his men, especially the young midshipmen entrusted to his nurturing. Many of the young men did not appreciate his philosophy. Acting Midshipman Gustavus Fox, for one, asked Commodore Hull for a transfer out from under Percival's strict discipline and emphasis on classwork. Percival advised that Fox's father had appealed to him to care for his son and keep him out of mischief. Hull rejected the transfer request, to the obvious benefit of the youngster. Fox went on to a stellar naval career, serving as Abraham Lincoln's assistant secretary of the navy.

Acting Midshipman John Downes Jr. also requested a transfer out of the *Cyane*. Percival reminded Hull that he had recently received two letters from their mutual friend Captain John Downes Sr. "urging upon me a vigilant care of his son, and to keep him strictly to his studies and duty and allow him to visit the shore but seldom."[129] Young Downes stayed put.

The case of Midshipman John L. Worden demonstrates the paternal, caring side of Percival. When Mad Jack put together his original crew, he asked for Worden. "He is the son of an industrious farmer on the Banks of the Hudson," explained Percival. "He says he has no friends to aid him."[130] The secretary approved Percival's request, and Worden went on to meet Mad Jack's expectations, eventually making naval history. He commanded the ironclad *Monitor* in its famous duel with the South's *Merrimack*, later rising to the rank of admiral.

Another legendary Percival yarn, one of the most repeated tales in the old navy, traces to this cruise. Officers in the British garrison at Gibraltar became embroiled in an angry dispute over the courage of Americans. When the *Cyane* showed up, several of the younger British officers saw the answer at hand. Retelling of the story has obscured their unit's identity, but it appears that they came from either the "Blind Half Hundred," the West Kent regiment, or the "Bloody Eleventh" of Devonshire. The Brits rowed out to the ship and were received on board but declined to visit the captain's cabin. When Mad Jack appeared on deck, the senior man handed him a note demanding satisfaction on general grounds. Prior to accepting the challenge, Percival asked the British lieutenant for the names of every officer in his regiment, listed in order of rank and seniority. Mad Jack told his visitors that they would hear from him in short order and dismissed them.

Percival gathered his officers and declared that he would not permit the American colors to be insulted or himself bullied. Since the British had some twenty officers and *Cyane* had only a master commandant and four lieutenants, he would make all his midshipmen acting lieutenants to

Retired Captain John Percival in a photograph by J.W. Black, Boston.
Courtesy of U.S. Department of the Navy.

even the sides. The middies whooped approval, and a cartel went on shore under a flag.

Knowledge of the challenge astounded the British regimental commander and other officers unaware of the brashness of a few of their fellow officers. The foolhardy young officers obviously were unfamiliar with the combative nature of the *Cyane* commander. The local governor quickly interceded and saved the day placing all of the British officers under house arrest until the Americans left the next morning.

Almost two years after his return to the States, Percival received promotion to the lofty rank of captain, effective September 8, 1841. Captain was the highest U.S. Navy rank prior to the Civil War. During the age of sail, many Cape Cod mariners achieved rank and prestige in the merchant service. Percival became the only Cape Codder to rise to the top in the navy.

In 1843, the secretary assigned Mad Jack to the board for the examination of midshipmen, a task close to his heart. The board convened in Philadelphia, and when it completed its work, Percival sent a brief but considerate note to an old associate informing the man how his boy fared before the board:

> *Dear X—*
>
> *Your son has passed. Do you recollect our taking the Columbus out of dock? She just grazed.*
>
> *Yours truly,*
>
> *J Percival*[131]

As much as he enjoyed work related to the advancement of midshipmen, he continued to agitate for a ship. But there were more ranking officers than available ships. Finally, his reputation as an overall maritime expert provided an opening. On October 13, 1843, Acting Secretary David Henshaw gave Percival his most prestigious command. The famed USS *Constitution*, fifty-two guns, rested in disrepair at Norfolk. The naval constructor said that it would cost $70,000 to make it fit for sea. Henshaw, from Massachusetts and quite familiar with Percival's reputation for thrift, faced a dilemma. He could not afford the estimated cost and could not allow "Old Ironsides" to rot. He sensed that Mad Jack could resolve his problem. Percival reported to the Virginia yard in December, evaluated the vessel and declared that he could fit it out for an extended cruise at a cost of $10,000. Many questioned the low figure, but it met with Henshaw's approval. Percival had completed the task within budget by April and sailed the ship to New York to complete his 447-man crew.

On May 29, the *Constitution* left New York on an epic voyage. The first order of business was to deliver U.S. ambassador Henry A. Wise to his post in Brazil. Thereafter, Percival's orders directed him to the east coast of Africa and into the China seas. He was to return to the States as he saw fit. In the end, the old ship spent 495 days at sea and covered 52,371 miles, its only circumnavigation.

On July 24, the ship crossed the line touching off one of the most immortalized events of the voyage. Old hands anticipated a visit from His Oceanic Majesty King Neptune and the initiation of the "polliwogs," or those who had never crossed the equator. Ambassador Wise claimed diplomatic immunity but found it necessary to donate a bottle of whiskey to Neptune's exuberant court in order to avoid the ordeal. "The spirit of fun was now rife," recalled a lieutenant. "Shouts of laughter resounded from all parts of the ship."[132]

One person did not laugh, however. Wise's legation secretary, Mr. Sargent, hid in his room. Neptune's constables dragged him on deck and gave him added attention. When the scrubbers tossed him into the water tank, he grabbed old Percival and pulled him in. Mad Jack gave Sargent a good washing for his trouble. Sargent did not appreciate the honor, and at first chance, he protested so strongly with Washington authorities that the navy put a stop to the custom.

At Mozambique, several of the crewmen tested Mad Jack. Two dozen men went on shore leave, and most came back drunk. But several failed to return at all. The captain ordered an aide to ready his gig, while he put on "his fighting coat" and picked up a heavy cane. "I will show them how to obey orders," he bellowed. Percival found three of his drunken crew in a native hut. "You wont go off eh," he yelled. "I'll see," and he brought his cane down on one who managed to get away. Another, in attempting to escape, crawled between Percival's legs, and the captain made a horse of him, all the while whacking the man with his cane. The sailor broke away, and Percival chased him into the water, thrashing and ducking him. "A picture was drawn of this affair and sent to the President, with this Inscription. 'Mad Jack Percival getting *his* crew on board the Constitution in the Bay of Majunga, Island of Madagascar.'—This picture went all over the United States on the ship's arrival home in 1846. He was greatly beloved by all his officers and his crew."[133]

The USS *Constitution*, Captain John Percival commanding, leaving Hawaii for Mexico in December 1845. *Courtesy of Raymond A. Massey.*

Farther along at Nos Be, while walking along the beach, Percival spotted a huge log on the drift line. He directed the ship's carpenter to cut it in planks and use them to make a coffin. His age and health remained a concern, and if he died on the cruise, he wanted to be returned home in the coffin. Percival no doubt recalled that Lord Nelson kept a long box handy made out of the mainmast of a defeated French warship. When he succumbed at Trafalgar, Nelson's men carried him back to England in the coffin. Percival fared better. He survived the voyage and at the same time put the casket to good use. He filled it with Oriental curios, teas and silks, gifts for the folks at home. Once in Dorchester, he used the box as a horse trough in front of his home.

The most discussed incident on the trip took place at Touron Bay in Cochin China (now Vietnam). "Old Ironsides" came to anchor at the place early in May 1845. One of a group of visiting mandarins slipped a letter to Percival. The note came from a Christian missionary, Bishop Dominque Lefèbvre. The man said that the local authorities condemned him to be executed for proselytizing. Percival felt that he had an obligation to save a citizen of a nation bound to the United States by treaties and traditional friendship. Mad Jack led a well-armed party of eighty men on shore, posting men at intervals until he reached the chief mandarin's place. He left letters for Lefèbvre and the king. In the king's letter, he demanded the release of the Frenchman. He arrested three mandarins and carried them back to the ship as hostages. On the following day, Mad Jack reinforced his bargaining position by capturing three junks owned by the king.

A few days passed, and Percival released the hostages, who promised to go to the king and seek the missionary's release. On the following day, the three captured junks attempted to escape. Marines fired their muskets at the fleeing boats. A spirited chase and demonstration ensued, and the Americans managed to recapture all of the junks. Local soldiers fled before the marines. Whether any natives succumbed during the skirmish remains questionable. The next day, armed with a pistol, Percival alone forced his way onto a national brig, throwing its crew in fear and confusion as he checked the craft. Then, after more than two weeks of stalemate, he released the junks and readied his ship for departure.

Not too long after, the French government reported on the release of Lefèbvre. The French felt that the American intervention led to the favorable outcome. However, the incident later became a political issue when an American consul in Singapore exaggerated Percival's actions. More recently, the event received renewed attention due to the war in Vietnam. Historians and writers recalled Percival's earlier foray and described the affair as the first armed western intervention in what is now Vietnam.

In June, the *Constitution* visited Macao, China, and by September, it had made Manila. Two months later, the ship reached Oahu. The likelihood of war with Mexico required Percival to proceed to California. He made the Baja Peninsula in January 1846, remaining on station for three months. In April, the American commodore released "Old Ironsides," and it headed for Cape Horn and the east coast of South America. Late on September 26, 1846, Percival had his ship off the familiar three towers of Nauset Light, and on the next afternoon, he came to anchor off India Wharf in Boston. On October 1, 1846, Mad Jack left the quarterdeck of the venerated *Constitution*, some forty-nine years after entering on the fabled *Victory*. Adding to his legendary status is the fact that both his first and last naval vessels are national shrines and remain in commission to this day.

Percival went on leave until September 1855, awaiting orders. At that time, the department placed him on the reserved list. Mrs. Percival died in Dorchester on September 13, 1857. Five years later, on September 17, 1862,

John Percival grave and memorial tablet at the Ancient Cemetery, West Barnstable. *Courtesy of Scott Thompson.*

Mad Jack succumbed at Dorchester as well. Both are buried at the Ancient Cemetery in West Barnstable. A review of Percival's will tells a lot about the man. Among his many benevolent bequests, he left money for the West Barnstable almshouse, the West Barnstable grammar school teachers, the Warren Street Chapel school and the Children's Friend Society of Boston, as well as $1,000 to the Massachusetts General Hospital to "be invested as a permanent fund, and the interest and income thereof to be appropriated for a free bed or free beds—and, as this is the gift of a poor old sailor, preference shall always be given to mariners."[134]

CHAPTER 8

Lemuel Shaw

Lion on the Bench

Lemuel Shaw may be a less glamorous figure than the other three strong personalities from West Barnstable's past. His renown is more or less limited to the legal field. Yet the case can be made that his influence is more lasting. Born in the former parsonage on what is now Church Street in the village on January 9, 1781, he went on to become a giant in the American judiciary.

The family in America descends from Abraham Shaw, who came to the colonies from Halifax, England, in 1636. His grandson, Joseph, farmed and milled in East Bridgewater, Massachusetts, and managed to put four sons through Harvard College. Each became a Congregational minister. One of the sons, John, held the ministry in South Bridgewater and married the daughter of another minister. Three of this couple's five sons became ministers, and a daughter had a son who became a preacher. One of John's boys who did not enter the ministry nonetheless sired two sons who did. "Thus in three generations did the family tree of Joseph the miller bear the fruit of ten ministers on one branch."[135]

Oakes Shaw, one of John's five boys, was born in 1736 and graduated from Harvard in 1758. He became pastor of the West Parish in Barnstable in 1760, serving until his death at seventy-one years of age. His first wife, Elizabeth Weld, daughter of an Attleboro, Massachusetts minister, died in 1772. Oakes and Elizabeth had three daughters. In 1774, Oakes married his second wife, Susanna Hayward of Braintree, Massachusetts. The couple had two sons, born at the parsonage in West

The Shaw parsonage on Church Street, 1892. *Private collection.*

Barnstable, Lemuel being the youngest. Considering the Shaw family history, everyone expected that young Lemuel would complete Harvard and enter the ministry.

His early learning relied on instruction provided by his father. Barnstable provided a narrow form of public education as early as 1683. By the late eighteenth century, the town employed a moving or so-called squadron system of schooling. Under this approach, a teacher would travel from settlement to settlement offering lessons in available dwellings. This approach enabled Lemuel's contemporaries to study the rudiments of basic subjects. Young John Percival Jr., by way of example, attended such classes for a total of nine months, fairly standard for the period. But Oakes and Susanna Shaw wanted much more for Lemuel. And since ministers were among the best educated and commonly served as local teachers, Oakes naturally took it on himself to prepare his son for college.

Finances proved a continuing concern for Reverend Shaw and his family throughout Lemuel's youth. In time, the minister and his wife found it necessary to grow rye for sale in Boston. While Susanna brought some assets to the marriage, Oakes's beginning salary of eighty pounds per annum was not sufficient to meet the Shaws' needs. The twenty cords of firewood that parishioners provided helped. But by 1784, circumstances forced the elder Shaw to borrow money for living expenses. In March, he protested, and at a meeting, the church members agreed to do better. Abraham Williams of Sandwich was a lender, and in discussing the note he held, he reacted to the community's intent in a letter to the minister. "I have been greatly concerned," he said, "lest you would be obliged to leave...for a want of a necessary Support; but now as they appear disposed to support you in the Ministry, to rectify past Wrongs—and do you justice for the future,—I hope you will soon be able to Discharge this & every Debt, and no more be obliged to pay 6. or 5. or any Interest to any Person."[136]

The problem persisted, however. Ten years later, the membership responded to their pastor's continuing pleas, declaring that "it was their mind that on the whole there was not anything due him, as he always said he was willing to suffer his proportion with the people." Two years after, an exasperated Oakes Shaw wrote, "God only knows the apprehension of my mind, the agitation, the great perplexity and trouble I have often had in attempting to obtain nearly what I was encouraged to hope for when I first became the Pastor of this flock, and how shockingly my feelings have been hurt."[137] His grandson, Lemuel Savage Shaw, wrote about his grandfather's "chronic remonstrance against what he conceived to be the unfairness with which he was treated by the people of the Precinct in money matters, leading almost to an open rupture."[138]

The continuing compensation problem may have played a role in the parents' decision in 1795 to send Lemuel to live with his mother's relatives in Braintree. In addition, the father began to doubt his ability to prepare his son for Harvard. Susanna's brother, Dr. Lemuel Hayward, took in young Shaw and arranged for a recent graduate of the college to instruct him for several months. The plan fell short when in the summer of 1796 Harvard rejected Lemuel's first application. Dr. Hayward regrouped, and later in the summer, the school approved Shaw's second application.

Shaw found it difficult to visit home while in school. In his first year, one trip took a full week to complete. The packet fought contrary winds all the

The West Parish meetinghouse, 2011. *Private collection.*

way to Barnstable, while unfavorable weather delayed his return by two days. And the constant problem with pay continued to plague Reverend Shaw. In his junior year, Lemuel asked his parents for $33.39 to discharge some bills. His mother admonished him for a lack of prudence and told him to apply to Dr. Hayward for the funds, "as your father has no money, and knows not when he will have any."[139] By no means did Shaw expect to live off others. After his freshman year, he taught at a Lexington school during vacations and accompanying leaves. He received $16.00 plus transportation and board for a ten-week term. Despite these commonplace challenges, Shaw graduated in 1800 with Phi Beta Kappa honors, uncertain of his future but leaning toward teaching as a career.

He taught for a brief period in one of the Boston public schools but before long had moved on to become an assistant editor at the *Boston Gazette*, a Federalist-leaning newspaper. Shaw spent much time at Uncle Hayward's home and, while there, became acquainted with two lawyers, Thomas O. Selfridge and David Everett. This association turned Shaw's mind toward the law, and in 1801, he began legal studies in Everett's office. Entering as a law student in an attorney's office was the only way to study law at the time. Law schools did not exist. Upon completing a three-year course with an experienced lawyer, a student would be admitted to practice before the Court of Common Pleas. Following two years of practice at that level, a student would be admitted to the Supreme Judicial Court bar. Before being admitted to full practice, the system required another two years of lawyering. Thus, an aspiring counselor prepared for seven years.

Everett removed to Amherst, New Hampshire, in 1802, and Shaw followed to carry on his studies. He continued to write on the side. The local newspaper, the *Farmers' Cabinet*, welcomed his contributions, including poetry. Nancy Melvill of the village also welcomed his company. She was the daughter of Major Thomas Melvill, a prominent leader in Boston during the Revolutionary era. The couple engaged to be married. Shortly thereafter, Nancy died. For the rest of his life, Shaw preserved two loving letters sent to him by his Nancy. He did not become betrothed again until 1818. On the positive side, in the fall of 1804, the Hillsborough County, New Hampshire, Court of Common Pleas admitted Shaw to practice at the court. Little over two months later, the Plymouth, Massachusetts Court of Common Pleas admitted Shaw as an attorney of that court.

Shaw set up his first office on Congress Street in Boston. In little over a year, late in 1806, he moved to State Street and entered the office of his old acquaintance Selfridge. Before long, Selfridge became involved in a silly but tragic dispute over a caterer's bill for a Democratic-Republican dinner. Benjamin Austin served as committee chairman of the event. Acting for the unhappy caterer, Selfridge initiated legal action against the committee. The parties quickly resolved the dispute, but hard feelings lingered. As a result, Selfridge took out a newspaper ad vilifying Austin and began carrying a pistol. Austin issued a veiled threat before his eighteen-year-old son, Charles, wielding a heavy cane, confronted Selfridge. Whether young Austin struck before Selfridge fired is uncertain. What is clear is that the gunshot mortally wounded Charles. The authorities charged Selfridge with manslaughter. Shaw made a brief appearance at his trial as a defense witness. The jury found the defendant not guilty. The verdict stirred warm political passions in town, and Selfridge departed for New York, leaving Shaw on his own.

For the first few years, Shaw labored over minor cases. In fact, his first argument before the Supreme Court did not occur until six years following his admission to practice in the Court of Common Pleas. The issue involved a five-dollar dispute. He lost the case. In 1811, he began to gain influence and attention by giving public speeches. He delivered his first discourse at the annual meeting of the Humane Society of Massachusetts. Shaw's growing stature became apparent in 1815 when Boston selected him to give the annual Fourth of July oration at Faneuil Hall, a prestigious engagement. Boston had elected him a representative to the General Court for four years beginning in 1811. He returned to the House for 1820 and moved to the Massachusetts Senate in 1821 and 1822. In 1829, he went back to the House for another year.

Shaw became active in the Federalist Party when it exerted great influence over the politics of the War of 1812. The party dominated in Massachusetts and southern New England at the time. It opposed the Jefferson-Madison administrations and the embargoes and war at every turn and also advocated for states' rights. In 1812, party stalwarts in Boston formed a chapter of the Washington Benevolent Society, an organization that fronted for the Federalists. Shaw played a major role in the activities of the association.

On the domestic side, in 1818 Shaw married Elizabeth Knapp, daughter of a successful Boston merchant. Like his father, he suffered the misfortune of losing his first wife after a relatively short marriage. Elizabeth died four years after their wedding. The couple, however, had two children: John Oakes and Elizabeth. Shaw remained a widower until 1827, when he married Hope Savage, daughter of Barnstable's Dr. Samuel Savage. This union also produced two children: Lemuel Jr. and Samuel Savage Shaw. Lemuel's daughter, Elizabeth, married Herman Melville, the famed author. Melville was the nephew of Nancy Melvill, Shaw's first betrothed from his days in Amherst. Melville dedicated his novel *Typee* to his father-in-law. Shaw's extended relationship with the author's family helps explain Melville's connection to Mad Jack Percival. Shaw and Percival were lifelong friends.

During his early years in Boston, Shaw served the town in a number of minor offices. Of most importance, along with Daniel Webster and others, he represented the town in the Constitutional Convention of 1820–21. While a number of issues took up the attention of the gathering, the principal change made it possible for Boston to incorporate as a city. Shaw played a key role in the matter, laying a foundation for his ultimate interest and expertise in the field of municipal law. In the months previous, he served as a Boston selectman.

Under the New England form of local government, decades in the making, an open meeting of all voters performed the legislative function of a town. Administrative and day-to-day management of municipal affairs rested in a board of selectmen, usually consisting of three members. Shaw advocated amending the state constitution so Boston could change to a more efficient and representative form. With some forty thousand inhabitants and up to nine thousand voters, town meetings could become unwieldy if too many attended. Just as worrisome, when the matters before a meeting did not generate popular excitement, only a handful of townsmen decided for the whole.

Boston recognized the problem as early as 1784, but five attempts to modernize failed. As authorized by the recent constitutional amendment, Boston appointed a committee in 1821 to "remedy the present evils."[140] Shaw served on the committee, which reported on the last day of the year. Town meeting debated the report's findings and recommendations for three days before adopting the committee's proposal by a wide margin. A petition for change went to the General Court, where Shaw as a member of the Committee on Towns shepherded it through the legislative mill. The legislature passed the measure, and in March 1822, the town accepted the act, making Boston a city. Shaw assumed a substantial share of the attendant work, drawing up the act of incorporation and drafting the greater part of the new charter.

Up to this point, Shaw was unknown on the national stage. Influential members of the community urged him to run for Congress, a post seemingly his for the asking. He declined, not wanting anything to do with the Washington scene. Benefiting from his position as president of the Suffolk Bar Association, he desired to remain focused on his growing law practice. Things began to change in July 1830.

Chief Justice Isaac Parker of the Massachusetts Supreme Judicial Court died suddenly at the age of sixty-two. Governor Levi Lincoln needed to find a replacement. An unwritten rule, broken only once, would promote the senior associate justice to the chief's post. Not bound by the custom, Lincoln looked elsewhere. And he did not have far to look. Lincoln knew Shaw from their days at Harvard. The two served together in the legislature

Lemuel Shaw profile. *Private collection.*

and the Constitutional Convention. Lincoln understood the requirements of the post better than many governors since he sat on the Supreme Judicial Court in 1824 before his gubernatorial run. And he appreciated Shaw's thoroughness and temperament. Lincoln checked with Daniel Webster, who enthusiastically endorsed the idea. The governor asked Webster to make the offer and urge its acceptance.

Webster went to Shaw's in the evening and presented the offer. Webster remembered that Shaw "was almost offended at the suggestion. 'Do you suppose,' said he, 'that I am going at my time of life to take an office that has so much responsibility attached to it for the paltry sum of three thousand dollars a year?'"[141] Webster used every conceivable argument. Early the next day, Shaw absolutely declined. Upon learning about the rejection, the governor sent a note back to Webster: "My Dear Sir,—I feel entirely overwhelmed by the difficulty which your communication presents, and will call upon you in fifteen minutes at your study."[142]

After his talk with Webster, the governor sent an appeal to Shaw. Webster followed up with several visits. "I plied him in every possible way," said

Webster, "and had interview after interview with him. He smoked and smoked, and, as I entreated and begged and expostulated, the smoke would come thicker and faster. Sometimes he would make a cloud of smoke so thick that I could not see him. I guess he smoked a thousand cigars while he was settling the point. He would groan and smoke. He declared, by all that was sacred, that he would resist the tempter."[143]

Once Webster left, Shaw resorted to form. He drew up a brief or memorandum as he labeled the paper. He then set down all the reasons against accepting the nomination followed by a more lengthy set of arguments in favor. Other members of the bar interceded, and in the end, Shaw reluctantly agreed to serve. His commission is dated August 30, 1830, and he took his seat during the September term in Berkshire County. Years later, Webster declared, "Massachusetts is indebted to me for one thing, if for nothing else. I have been the cause of giving her a chief-justice to her highest court for more than a quarter of a century one unsurpassed in every thing that constitutes an upright learned and intelligent judge. Massachusetts is indebted to me for having Judge Shaw at the head of her judiciary for thirty years; for he never would have taken the place had it not been for me."[144]

This is not the place to present a scholarly review of Justice Shaw's judicial philosophy and important decisions. Two books fit for popular consumption already do the job and cannot be improved on. Professor Leonard W. Levy in his *The Law of the Commonwealth and Chief Justice Shaw* and Judge Elijah Adlow with *The Genius of Lemuel Shaw* review at length the work of Shaw. During his thirty years on the high bench, "he was a prodigious worker…writing more opinions than any other justice in the court's history, many of which were regarded then, and remain today, landmarks in American jurisprudence (more than 2,200 opinions in total with only a handful of dissents, spread throughout 56 volumes of *The Massachusetts Reports*, along with 55 volumes of manuscript notes on every case to come before the court)."[145] One must keep in mind that during the Shaw era, the Supreme Judicial Court served both as a capital trial court and an appellate court.

Although some of the issues handled by the Shaw court had broad implications, they garnered little notice beyond the legal community. The new nation was undergoing great change and growth. The transformation required interpretation and application of the common law, always in a state of flux, as well as matters involving procedural due process. To this day, legal scholars generally agree that what U.S. Chief Justice John Marshall did for constitutional law, Shaw did for the nation's common law. Judicial review of the legislative power also took up much of the time of the Shaw court. Not to be overlooked, the court from time to time ruled on the essence of and bounds to the judicial power. Among the many negligence issues resolved, a landmark 1850 ruling settled the question of responsibility for damaging consequences of a non-negligent and unintentional action. The industrialization of the country changed the process of contracting, and the related laws required much construction and interpretation. Municipal governments were evolving and growing, leading to the need to define their roles, powers and jurisdictions. Likewise, matters involving the growth and expansion of railroads repeatedly appeared before the Shaw court.

A few of the trials he presided over generated considerable excitement due to the sensational nature of the cases. Shaw earned the lasting admiration of the Roman Catholic bishop of Boston for his fair handling of the Ursuline Convent trial of 1834, even though the outcome disappointed the church. An atmosphere of religious prejudice prevailed in the locality at the time, leading to rumors that the convent held a woman against her will and that the place was unfit for human habitation. On the night of August 11, a mob broke into and burned the convent to the ground. The gang returned the next night to destroy the gardens and orchards. Authorities arrested thirteen for arson and burglary, including John R. Buzzell, the ringleader. The prosecutor pleaded that since Roman Catholics would testify, potential jurors should be asked if they would believe Catholics even under oath. Shaw refused to use the question or similar irrelevant questions. In the end, Buzzell and eleven others received acquittals. A sixteen-year-old boy was convicted of book burning.

Perhaps the most famous capital trial Shaw handled was the Webster-Parkman case. George Parkman was a well-to-do Bostonian. John W. Webster served as a chemistry professor at Harvard's Medical School. The two maintained a friendship to the extent that in 1842 Webster secured a loan from Parkman. Five years later, with his loan unpaid and still in financial distress, Webster obtained another loan from Parkman. Parkman secured the loans by a mortgage on Webster's personal property, including a collection of rare minerals. In arrears on his loans, in 1849, Webster acquired a loan from Parkman's brother-in-law using the minerals as security. Parkman learned of the duplicity, denounced Webster and demanded a settlement of the indebtedness owed him.

The two men agreed to meet at the Medical School. Parkman went to the school and disappeared. People close to him offered rewards for information about his whereabouts. Then Dr. Webster's behavior at his laboratory aroused the suspicion of a janitor. The man made a secret search of Webster's workplace and found the remains of a human body, later identified as being that of Parkman. A grand jury indicted Webster for murder. The case became a national sensation.

Evidence offered at the eleven-day trial created a circumstantial chain indicating guilt. Webster addressed the jury, never admitting guilt. Then Shaw delivered a memorable charge to the jury that became a precedent followed repeatedly in murder trials thereafter. Shaw spent considerable time clearly explaining the concept of reasonable doubt, as well as the matter of circumstantial evidence. Relative to this case, his biographer said of Shaw's emulated performance, "No greater tribute can be afforded to a judicial utterance than that it shall be adopted and quoted universally upon occasions where need arises for explanation of the principles expounded."[146]

The jury found Webster guilty, and some newspapers and observers outside of Massachusetts heaped abuse on Shaw, blaming him for an injustice. However, criticism came to an end in 1850 when Webster applied for a pardon on the grounds of his innocence. The governor rejected the request. Webster sent another petition seeking a commutation. This time, he made a full admission of guilt, arguing that premeditation was not involved. He said that Parkman taunted and abused him to the point he lost his temper. The Executive Council and the governor did not believe the excuse, and they rejected his plea. The difficult task of sentencing Webster to death fell to the chief justice. But since his critics based their disparagement on a belief in Webster's innocence, now disproved, criticism of Shaw faded away.

Shaw's involvement with fugitive slave laws also led to some condemnation of his judicial actions. From a personal perspective, he despised everything about slavery. As early as 1811, he spoke out against the practice. In his speech to the Humane Society, he called slavery "one continued series of tremendous crimes."[147] In 1836, he ruled in favor of a slave girl named Med. Her owner carried her to the free state of Massachusetts from a slave state in the South. When the mistress prepared to return to the South with Med, abolitionists took legal action to determine her status in the Commonwealth. Shaw ruled that she did not flee, so the fugitive slave laws did not apply, and the Massachusetts laws prohibiting slavery protected the young woman once in the state. Similar cases in 1841 and 1844 resulted in the same finding and high praise from the many abolitionists in the region.

On the other hand, in 1851, the case of an escaped slave named Sims appeared in Shaw's court. About to be returned to Georgia, sympathetic Massachusetts supporters sought his release through a writ of habeas corpus. Shaw denied the writ, declaring the Fugitive Slave Act to be constitutional and controlling. Shaw's written decision showed "the workings of an absolutely honest legal mind, moving to an inevitable conclusion…Another judge with his strong opinions on slavery, living in the abolitionist atmosphere of New England, would perhaps consciously or subconsciously have found a way, either upon the main controversy or upon collateral issues, to free the slave. But Shaw's mind ran true."[148] A later member of the court who disagreed with the ruling likewise said, "The Chief Justice was so simple, honest, upright, and straightforward, it never occurred to him there was any way around, over, under, or through the barriers of the Constitution—that is the only apology that can be made for him."[149] The abolitionists were not as kind. They vilified Shaw.

In the same way Shaw's rulings held sway, Shaw the man overawed those in his presence. A rather large man with a brusque manner, a deep bass voice, piercing eyes and shaggy head of hair, he appeared an imposing figure. While watching a sculptor shape a statue of a lion, Rufus Choate, a prominent Boston attorney, observed, "Why that's the best likeness of Chief Justice Shaw that I ever saw."[150]

Benjamin Butler described the man by way of a tale. Butler owned "an immense mastiff, with a black muzzle, very quiet but very powerful." Intending to deliver the animal to a friend, he boarded the Lowell–Boston cars and met a salute.

"Halloa, halloa, Butler, where are you going this morning?"

"Down to the Supreme Court, gentlemen."

"Is that your dog?"

"Yes."

"What are you taking him down to court for?"

"Oh, I thought I would show him the chief justice so as to teach him to growl."

Shortly thereafter, in the course of business, Butler found that Shaw possessed a dry sense of humor. The chief justice had recently handed down an opinion favoring Butler. After perfunctory greetings, Shaw said, "Well. Mr. Butler, you won your Charlestown case?"

"'Oh' replied the attorney, 'thanks, Mr. Chief Justice; I am exceedingly obliged to you for giving me that case.'"

"'Well, then, Mr. Butler,' said Shaw, 'I take it you have no fault to find with that last growl of the chief justice.'"[151]

Shaw resigned his post in August 1860. Over the decades, many leaders of the bar have praised his performance in office. The testimonials follow a pattern. Oliver Wendell Holmes Jr., the great associate justice

Lemuel Shaw. *Private collection.*

of the U.S. Supreme Court and once chief justice of the Massachusetts Supreme Judicial Court, summarized the widespread admiration when he endorsed the view that Shaw was "the greatest *magistrate* which this country has produced."[152] Along the same line, while at Harvard Law, Felix Frankfurter, a future great associate justice of the U.S. Supreme Court, received an offer to serve on the Massachusetts high court. After much

LEMUEL SHAW
CHIEF JUSTICE SUPREME JUDICIAL COURT. 1830-1860
BORN. WEST BARNSTABLE. 1781   DIED. BOSTON. 1861
PRESENTED 1915 TO THE COUNTY OF BARNSTABLE BY HIS GRANDDAUGHTER
JOSEPHINE MacC SHAW

Bust of Chief Justice Shaw, overlooking the bench in the Superior Court, Barnstable. *Courtesy of John Burke.*

reflection, he declined the offer, prompting friend Tom Powell to ask why he even considered accepting. Frankfurter explained, "I said—I think very quietly—'Tom, I didn't think that a place that had been occupied by Lemuel Shaw and Oliver Wendell Holmes Jr. was beneath me, or too meager for my powers.'"[153]

In 1915, his granddaughter, Miss Josephine MacC. Shaw of Boston presented Barnstable County with a bust of Shaw. The bust rests above the bench in the Superior Courthouse. The news account reporting the gift described Shaw as "one of the greatest jurists that has ever lived among the English speaking nations of the world."[154] A year later, the Massachusetts and Boston Bar Associations placed a commemorative tablet in the front of the old Shaw parsonage on Church Street. The slate tablet is affixed to a fieldstone "as solid as the chief justice's character and as secure as his fame."[155] The memorial has the added importance of fronting the only surviving birthplace of any of West Barnstable's celebrated four.

Due to its historical significance, the homestead merits some discussion. Flimsy tradition suggests that one John Jenkins built the structure before 1685. But tradition is an unreliable source. Documentary evidence and the building itself indicate construction at a much later date. John Jenkins died in 1684, having spent much of his life on a plantation of Barnstable that is now a part of Falmouth. As the venerable historian Amos Otis revealed, Jenkins probably never lived for a lengthy period within the bounds of the present town of Barnstable. His son Joseph did reside in West Barnstable, but at some distance from Church Street (then Sandy Street). He had two sons, Joseph Jr. and Benjamin. Born in 1707, Benjamin married in 1730. Benjamin is important because he is the first Jenkins to be associated by record to the building's site. Barnstable Probate Court Book 2, page 131 shows that he sold the home to Oakes Shaw in August 1763. The absence of an earlier recorded owner suggests that Benjamin was the original owner. Moreover, the basic structure is a relatively modern two-story Cape initially associated with the first half of the eighteenth century. Remember, just a few decades before 1685, many local houses were crude one-room shanties or primitive booths. There is a likelihood that Benjamin built the dwelling at a date close to his 1730 wedding. In any event, there is no known evidence to support the "prior to 1685" tradition.

In defense of this kind of exaggeration, the practice is harmless and not uncommon here and elsewhere. To illustrate, not too many years ago, the town acquired an old dwelling near Sacrament Rock. When the town put the place on the market, it publicized the longstanding, traditional claim that the building traced to 1640. Local historians scoffed at the assertion. Upon review, the town set 1740 as the year of construction.

According to her grandson, Lemuel's mother Susanna "was enabled to buy the house and add to its comforts through some slight patrimony of

The Shaw parsonage, 1970. *Private collection.*

her own." Her father, Captain John Hayward, died in 1773. The grandson added, "It was to this excellent wife and mother that the family owed all its little measure of thrift and prosperity."[156] There is some indication that Oakes lived in the dwelling before his marriage, but there is little proof that he alone ever had the means to purchase the place. Oakes died in 1807, and his widow continued to live in the homestead. During the height of the War of 1812, Lemuel, concerned for her safety, had her remove to his home in Boston. She thereupon rented the farm to several parties, including Levi Goodspeed. In Goodspeed's rental agreement, Mrs. Shaw instructed Goodspeed to "keep the fences in good repair and do this labour etc. at his own expense and…not to carry any manure off the said place."[157] Before

The dooryard of the Shaw parsonage, 1970. *Private collection.*

she died in 1839 at her son's place in Boston, Susanna Shaw sold the home to Jesse Crosby, who in turn sold it back to the chief justice. In August 1851, Shaw sold the old home to David Parker. Not until the 1950s did the place again serve as a parsonage for the West Parish. Two decades later, it went back to private hands and since has passed through several different owners.

Chief Justice Shaw died on March 29, 1861, less than a year after his retirement and eighteen months before the passing of his childhood friend John Percival. He is buried at the Mount Auburn Cemetery, Cambridge.

CHAPTER 9
The Following Years

W ith the passing of Lemuel Shaw and John Percival, West Barnstable's place on the national stage ended. The village reverted to its original status as a pastoral New England hamlet. This remained the case until the last quarter of the twentieth century, when residential development spread to some of the quiet woodlands and former farmlands of the community. A vigorous public-private campaign initiated in the 1960s eventually preserved much of the wild lands, placing considerable village acreage in permanent protection. The so-called West Barnstable Conservation Lands, a 1,114-acre wooded area in the southwest sector of the village, is the second-largest protected area in the town of Barnstable after the more than 2,560 preserved acres of the Great Marshes. Of course, half of the latter holdings are in West Barnstable, as is half of the more than 900 protected acres on Sandy Neck. The 300-acre Bridge Creek Conservation Area and the 110-acre Otis-Atwood parcel are other substantial parts of the village that will remain undisturbed by development. Numerous lesser conservation lands, some administered by private entities such as land trusts, add to the fact the village is made up of an unusually high percentage of protected land.

While West Barnstable now leads the town in preserving open space, in the early years, it led the town in preserving people. The town began operating an almshouse or poor farm in West Barnstable in 1769. For some three hundred years, responsibility for the poor rested with the towns in Massachusetts. In 1642, the court at Plymouth issued a decree to this end, duplicating the outline of the 1601 Elizabethan Poor Law of England. In

Oil painting of Sandy Neck by Robert P. Wheeler. *Private collection.*

the early years, towns handled the matter by auctioning services of the poor. Beginning in 1722, Barnstable showed interest in constructing a building dedicated to housing the indigent. Townsmen debated the topic from time to time. A development in 1754 moved the issue forward. Village resident Parker Lombard died and left his real estate to the town to be "hired out to the highest Bidder by those Persons that the Town shall appoint from time to time and the Rent or Income shall be improved for the Use & Benefit of the Poor of the Town of Barnstable from one Generation to another and never to be sold."[158]

Lombard's real estate consisted of a house and comparatively narrow strip of land composed of forty-eight acres running northerly from the upper reaches of Boat Cove Creek all the way to the Great Marshes. Lombard's dwelling, situated at the southern end of his parcel, apparently served as the town's first almshouse. In 1766, the town appointed a committee to consider whether to repair or replace the building. The committee recommended tearing down and replacing the house. But the townspeople rejected the suggestion. Two years later, another committee

The rear of the Barnstable Poor Farm, 1968. *Private collection.*

made the same proposal. This time, the town agreed with the plan, and Benjamin Hamblen set about building a one-story almshouse twenty-six feet square along the west side of what is now Meetinghouse Way and one-fifth of a mile north of the present fire station. The town accepted the structure in January 1769 and placed John Crocker Jr. in charge. Barnstable replaced this house with a larger version in 1821.

Institutions of this type at the time housed all classes of needy, including vagrants, orphans, insane and able-bodied poor in general. In 1843, reform advocate Dorothea L. Dix investigated Massachusetts poorhouses. Her explosive report to the legislature, denounced at first, resulted in improvements to the system. Dix visited the West Barnstable

The Barnstable Poor Farm viewed from the north, 1968. *Private collection.*

facility and found "[f]our females in pens and stalls. Two chained certainly. I think all."[159]

By 1915, the 171 almshouses or poorhouses in Massachusetts had evolved to the point that they were considered municipal infirmaries similar to modern nursing homes. Initially called the Town's House, the Barnstable place went under many names—from almshouse to poorhouse, poor farm, Lombard Home and Town Infirmary. From time to time, the town added to the second structure, including a two-story northern ell, a smaller southern ell, barns and sheds. As late as 1945, the site housed fourteen residents. In less than two more decades, Barnstable and other Massachusetts towns relinquished responsibility for maintaining such facilities. For a few years, the town rented the place as a regular residence. In 1967, a town committee studied the feasibility of preserving the historically and architecturally significant place. The committee recommended restoration of the basic or central structure and the best of the barns. The report generated little enthusiasm, and under local pressure to turn the grounds to open space, the town demolished the deserted facility in 1972.

Percival and Shaw lived to see a pronounced change to their little West Barnstable. Outside forces disturbed the tranquility of the village just before Christmas in 1853. The Cape Cod Branch Rail Road reached Sandwich in 1848. An extension to Hyannis became the next goal. However, a difference of opinion arose. Some interests wanted a south-side route through Marstons Mills, Osterville and Centerville. The *Patriot* sided with those who advocated a route through West Barnstable, Barnstable village and Yarmouth village, arguing that the level path along the north shore would prove less expensive. The paper felt that in the end "it will be the means of affording to the citizens of the Cape towns, those rapid facilities for communicating with Boston and other cities, which their isolated situation and peculiar business pursuits, render so very necessary and desirable to them."[160] The final decision favored the northern route. And early in 1853, the *Patriot* reported, "We are happy to be able to chronicle the fact that the work of extending the Cape Cod Branch Rail Road is steadily progressing."[161]

The line reached West Barnstable at the end of the year on December 22. Before moving along to Barnstable in May, the enterprise changed its name to the Cape Cod Railroad Company. When it finally reached Hyannis in early July 1854, the company celebrated with a public clambake, providing free food for anyone. The first West Barnstable train station opened in 1854. The New York, New Haven and Hartford Railroad Company constructed a replacement in 1911. This building still stands. The location of the station and a post office necessarily nearby promoted the growth of a central business district in the general area. While the twentieth century witnessed some sprawl, the neighborhood is still considered the heart of the village.

"A boom in real estate," pronounced the *Patriot* in the spring of 1889. "Two new buildings building at one time: one a town building and one a stable…Keep on until we get a public hall and library, then West Barnstable will be an attractive place in winter as well as summer."[162] The one-and-a-half-story town building measured twenty-two by twenty-eight feet, designed as a municipal office. The selectmen/assessors became the primary tenants. For years, they agitated for a new office. The selectmen designed the building and managed the construction, working with an original appropriation of

The Old Selectmen's Office, 1968. *Private collection.*

$1,000 and several modest supplements. The local newspaper congratulated them on their success, adding that "if the building is not just what is needed it is their own fault."[163] The location, relatively isolated from the town's business and population centers, can be explained. In the years prior to occupying the new office, the three-member board of selectmen held its monthly meetings just down the hill in the poorhouse. Free meals provided by the keeper enticed them to meet at his place, and locating the new office nearby allowed for the continuation of the dining custom.

The town conducted its administrative business at this location beginning in June 1889 and running until 1926, when a much larger office opened in Hyannis at a cost of $85,000. In the years since the move to Hyannis, the town has found a number of uses for the West Barnstable building known as the Old Selectmen's Office. The Boy Scouts occupied it for a while, and it now serves as a seasonal art gallery. For long periods, however, the place remained vacant, and this led to problems. By 1963, the unoccupied building was showing signs of serious disrepair, including a decaying roof, broken windows and peeling paint. The West Barnstable Historical Society initiated a restoration project, the first of several over recent years.

Supportive of the effort, Walter Muir Whitehill, the late Boston historian, considered the building a quaint and fine example of the shingle style of architecture that prevailed during the 1870s and 1880s along the New England coast. Painted olive green, the warm texture of the shingles served to emphasize the surface instead of the skeleton and demonstrated a longing for the sea. After rejecting a measure to fund simple repairs several years earlier, the regular town meeting in March 1964 appropriated $1,500 for the task. A development during the previous September piqued interest in the old building.

In order to estimate the cost of basic repairs for inclusion in the funding request, the local society's president secured the key to the then abandoned building. In 1899, the town fathers bought a ladder for $1.50 to enable them to reach the attic. By 1963, the ladder was long gone. In fact, the main floor of the office was bare. But the condition of the roof could not be determined without a close inspection. The president brought in a ladder, reached the attic and made a remarkable discovery. Original town records dating back to the beginning of the nineteenth century littered the attic floor, tossed around by the winds. The neatly penned March 1802 town meeting warrant of nineteen articles covering a range of issues from bounties on foxes, blackbirds and crows through herring river regulations to swine running at large was among the oldest documents. Others dealt with Jefferson's 1807 embargo, a War of 1812 public safety committee and a proposed smallpox hospital. The windblown find was gathered up in five large cartons and sent to the town archives.

Obliged to clean up the place as a condition for its use by his Scout troop, Harold Wheeler, village Scoutmaster in the 1940s, explained how the records made it to the attic: "My good wife helped me with the clean-up job. In the old cabinets and roll-top desks…were just all kinds of papers—deeds, town meeting warrants, petitions, reports, just about everything. Some of the stuff was scattered around the floor." He added, "We were filling up a small truck, headed for the dump with just plain rubbish, broken glass and so forth. But when it came to the old papers my wife and I thought it would be a shame to throw them out; someone might like to look at them someday. So, we put them upstairs in cartons and wooden boxes. It was a day's work up and down a ladder."[164] Two decades later, the Wheelers' good sense paid off.

A year after the selectmen's office went up, an inexpensive but (at the time) popular structure took shape in the hills of the village. Local travelers passing over the hilly spine between the north and south sides of town always marveled at the spectacular distant sights from Clay Hill, some 190 feet above sea level. Faraway objects such as Marconi's telegraph towers in Wellfleet came in view. A group got together, raised $200, gained permission from the owner of the peak and built an observatory in the form of a simple wooden tower 20 feet tall. Fourteen years later, the group made repairs to the tower and the primitive roadway leading from the town road through the woods to the top. The workers removed some stones by hand, but a number of boulders required the use of dynamite. Even so, repairs cost only $100. A participant wrote to the local newspaper, "[N]ow we have our beautiful view assured to us, we hope, for another succession of years."[165]

In 1903, the Commonwealth came to appreciate the view and took over the tower, making it a fire lookout. The site in the southeast corner of the village remained a favorite attraction, handling 2,355 visitors the first year under state operation. In 1919, the state replaced the old tower with a substantial metal structure. A news story for 1923 reported that the tower "had been visited by 1,600 persons this year. They came from 29 states and six foreign countries. Last year more than 1,800 persons found their way to the spot."[166]

When the builder set the foundation and constructed the chimney for the selectmen's office, he did not have to travel far for bricks. Commercial brickmaking on a small scale began in West Barnstable as early as 1846. The occupation became more organized in 1862 when the Charles H. Macomber Company took over the small business of E.S. Young. In 1878, Noah Bradford Jr., Benjamin Crocker, Charles Crocker and Levi Goodspeed began making bricks under the name of the West Barnstable Brick Company. James Eldridge acted as superintendent. In 1887, Abel D. Makepeace purchased the operation located along the marsh a quarter of a mile to the east of the site of the old Otis homestead. His firm sold the town the bricks for its office, put up some two miles to the west.

Makepeace remained at the helm during the peak years of the operation. By 1889, he employed twenty men and was turning out twenty-five thousand bricks daily. A small percentage of the bricks, something on the order of one in one hundred, were embossed with the words "W. Barnstable Brick Co." and today are considered collectable.

In 1925, Thomas H. Arden purchased the business. Within two years, the local newspaper reported that "Mr. Arden has spared no expense since taking over…to give not only the largest possible output, but has also enlarged his plant and equipped it with the latest and most up-to-date machinery, and has not only lessened the actual manual labor for the men employed, but has made the working conditions much more pleasant."[167] He turned out 100,000 bricks each working day, all embossed with a new "W.B.B." lettering.

Arden entertained many visitors, none more famous than Henry Ford. Touring the region in search of items for his historic Greenfield Village collections, Ford was attracted to a pair of antiquated surplus engines at the brick factory. Arden loaded them onto rail cars and shipped them to Ford's place in Dearborn, Michigan. "These pieces of machinery Mr. Ford tried hard to pay for but Mr. Arden had his way and the world's richest man took them as a gift, and cleared them out of space which could be used for something else."[168] A few days later, the Cape Cod Auto Company of Hyannis drove a new Fordson tractor to Arden's office, compliments of Mr. Ford.

The majority of workers at the brick factory were recent immigrants from Finland. Finns found their way to the American colonies as early as 1638. In the middle of the nineteenth century, most of the newly arrived Finns settled in the upper Midwest. By the latter part of the century, more and more were settling in Massachusetts cities such as Fitchburg, Worcester and Quincy. Before long, some found their way to the Cape. Albert Lundquist may have been the first Finn in Barnstable, arriving in 1885. John C. Makepeace remembered that his brother William had Russian Finns chopping wood for him in town around 1888. Many of the immigrants fled the heavy-handed policies of Russian tsar Nicholas II, who tried to dominate and rule the Grand Duchy of Finland without the consent of the Finns. The Russification of Finland stretched from 1899 to 1917. Even after Finns made it in America, enmity toward Russia held. A 1914 citizenship ceremony in the Barnstable courthouse demonstrated the point. After presiding over the swearing in of an older Finnish gentleman from West Barnstable, the judge inquired if he knew what the oath meant. "Ya," he answered, "it means the Czar can go to hell!"

At the outset, there were several sects of Finnish Lutherans in the village. Over time, evolution led to the single First Lutheran Church. The immigrant men and their sons constructed the building that was opened in 1924 and is still a vibrant presence in the village. The Finnish influence persisted beyond the early years. As late as 1955, some of the services here were performed in the Finnish language, although English otherwise prevailed.

An unused sauna, one of the last still standing in the village. *Private collection.*

In addition to chopping firewood and working at the brick factory, Finnish men worked on nearby cranberry bogs and dug clams in the harbor. A high percentage maintained a family cow, and everyone had a garden. Large families were the norm. A few men ran their own small, profitable dairy farms. Others turned to carpentry. Saunas, usually referred to simply as steam houses, dotted the village landscape. Surnames such as Pelton (or Peltonen), Syriala, Maki, Lahteine, Salo, Kaihlanen, Niskula, Wirtanen and Ruska seemed to blot out the old Yankee names, especially in the eastern half of West Barnstable. But the dominance of the Finnish population has passed. The oldest remaining are second-generation Finnish-Americans, and many have assimilated by marriage. Others have moved away. Sets of blond, blue-eyed youngsters no longer romp through the village fields, over the hills and along the byways as in yesteryears. Nonetheless, there can be little wonder why this part of the village is still affectionately referred to as Finntown.

Two major undertakings in the mid-twentieth century forever altered the character of the village. In 1947, the Commonwealth presented plans for a Mid-Cape Expressway running down the center of the peninsula from the

An 1892 view of the village from the area of the present westbound Exit 5 of the Mid-Cape Highway. *Private collection.*

Sagamore Bridge to Orleans. Constructed as a four-lane, median-separated freeway, work began in 1950 and crossed West Barnstable, ending for the time in 1953 in the southeast corner of the village at Route 132. The roadway assumed the Route 6 designation, while the old route that followed ancient ways closer to the bay gave up the label and became Route 6A. The new highway not only isolated the southern neighborhoods of the village from the main, but it also enhanced commercial and tourist traffic on and off the Cape. Scheduled passenger railroad service from the Cape to Boston soon ended, a victim of the popularity and convenience of the new highway.

The second project involved higher education. Cape Cod Community College, established in 1961, initially occupied the old Normal School

Entering Shark City on a roadway from Finntown. *Private collection.*

building in Hyannis. The college quickly outgrew the place and eyed a new facility for the West Barnstable woods near the Route 6/Route 132 interchange. The school moved to a new 116-acre campus at this location in 1970. Known as 4Cs, it is the only comprehensive college on the Cape east of the canal. The Massachusetts Maritime Academy is situated on the mainland side of the canal at Buzzards Bay. Some sticklers consider Buzzards Bay to be off-Cape, and therefore the academy cannot be considered a Cape college. The college in West Barnstable offers more than two dozen associate in arts degrees, seventeen associate in science degrees and provides forty-two career certificate programs. During a year, about eight thousand students take courses at the school. All told, the place is a busy corner of the village.

Approaching the end, one question remains. Why is the western half of West Barnstable called Shark City? Few residents have any idea. When an explanation is offered, it may vary altogether from another interpretation or recollection. The most repeated and colorful explanation involves the train station. In the early years of rail service, the West Barnstable stop served a substantial number of passengers traveling to or from the south shore villages of Cotuit, Marstons Mills, Osterville and Centerville. Horse-drawn conveyances carried the passengers between points. Layovers at West Barnstable became inevitable. And waiting travelers passed the time playing cards. Legend indicates that a handful of locals made the most of the opportunities offered and fleeced anyone gullible enough to engage them in games of poker. Thus, West Barnstable became the place of card sharks, or Shark City. This amounts to a good story that can be accepted or rejected at anyone's choice.

Traditional tales of this sort make up much of any locality's history. Traditions can be entertaining, but purists want facts. And when the facts are reviewed, it is apparent that West Barnstable has a unique and exemplary past largely due to four important people born in the village. All four reached the pinnacle in their fields. All four made major contributions to the nation's early development. James Otis Jr., a prominent lawyer, became the intellectual head of the American independence movement in New England. Much of his thinking made its way into our founding documents. His sister Mercy Otis Warren became an early and influential political activist, satirist, poet and historian, roles unheard of for a woman of the period. John Percival rose to the highest rank in the U.S. Navy, served in five wars, nurtured a host of future naval leaders and, for good measure, saved "Old Ironsides" from the scrapheap. Lemuel Shaw became the country's magistrate, interpreted the common law for years to come and set the highest standard for American jurists. There may be another little village somewhere able to match this crop, but one does not come to mind.

Notes

PREFACE

1. Palfrey, *Discourse Pronounced*, 28.

CHAPTER I

2. Sandborn, *Familiar Letters of Henry David Thoreau*, 431.
3. Dwight, *Travels in New England and New York*, 67.
4. Gross, *Lincoln's Own Stories*, 29.
5. Teal, *Life and Death of the Salt Marsh*, 24–25.
6. Swift, *Genealogical Notes of Barnstable Families*, 2:242.
7. *Barnstable Patriot*, October 18, 1881.
8. *Barnstable Patriot*, March 5, 1850.
9. Ibid.
10. *Barnstable Patriot*, July 11, 1849.
11. *Barnstable Patriot*, October 18, 1881.
12. *Barnstable Patriot*, March 19, 1889.
13. Nye, *Scientific Duck Shooting in Eastern Waters*, 10.
14. Tapply, *Sportsman's Notebook*, 258.
15. *Hyannis Patriot*, January 20, 1927.
16. Ibid.
17. *Hyannis Patriot*, October 30, 1930.

CHAPTER 2

18. Gookin, *Historical Collections of the Indians in New England*, vol. 1, 1ˢᵗ series, 148.
19. Frederick Freeman, *History of Cape Cod: Annals of Barnstable County* (Boston: Geo. C. Rand and Avery), 1:99.
20. Powell, "Archaeological Traverse of Sandy Neck," 4.
21. *Barnstable Patriot*, October 28, 1884.
22. Thoreau, *Cape Cod*, 86.
23. *Barnstable Patriot*, October 29, 1900.
24. *Barnstable Patriot*, August 21, 1922.
25. *Barnstable Patriot*, September 11, 1922.
26. *Barnstable Patriot*, October 16, 1922.
27. Trayser, *Barnstable*, 30.
28. Trayser, *Report of Proceedings*, 40.

CHAPTER 3

29. Bradford and Deane, *History of Plymouth Plantation*, 86.
30. Trayser, *Barnstable*, 10.
31. *Barnstable Patriot*, February 28, 1916.
32. Swift and Cogswell, *Barnstable Town Records*, 1.
33. Swift, *Genealogical Notes*, 1:490.
34. Ibid., 2:7.
35. *Barnstable Patriot*, November 11, 1884.
36. Swift and Cogswell, *Town Records*, 33.
37. Swift, *Genealogical Notes*, 1:462.

CHAPTER 4

38. Deyo, *History of Barnstable County*, 384.
39. *Province Laws (Resolves, etc.).*—1717–18, 3ʳᵈ Sess., Ch. 146, 575–76.
40. Swift and Cogswell, *Town Records*, 24.
41. Goehring, *West Parish Church of Barnstable*, 12.
42. Ibid., 34.
43. Thygeson, *Articles of Faith and Covenant*, 6.

44. Stowe, *Oldtown Fireside Stories*, 20.

45. Sinnott, *Meetinghouse & Church*, 41.

46. Swift and Cogswell, *Town Records*, 18.

47. *Barnstable Patriot*, November 3, 1830.

48. Parker, *Order of the Justice of the Peace*.

49. Trayser, *Barnstable*, 47.

Chapter 5

50. Swift, *Genealogical Notes*, 2:223.

51. Tudor, *Life of James Otis*, 6.

52. Fritz, *Cast for a Revolution*, 41.

53. Swift, *Genealogical Notes*, 2:223.

54. Tudor, *Life of James Otis*, xviii.

55. Sparks, *Library of American Biography*, 2nd ser., 2:16.

56. Fritz, *Cast for a Revolution*, 82.

57. Marshall, *History of the Colonies of North America*, 351.

58. Ridpath, *James Otis*, 9.

59. Tudor, *Life of James Otis*, 57.

60. Quincy, *Reports of Cases Superior Court*, 421.

61. Grinnell, "James Otis, Jr.," 52.

62. Ferling, *John Adams*, 24.

63. McCullough, *John Adams*, 49.

64. Adams, Letter to William Tudor, 4.

65. Tudor, *Life of James Otis*, 63.

66. Ibid., 63–64.

67. Ibid., 66–67.

68. Ibid., 67.

69. Ibid., 68.

70. Ibid., 68–69.

71. Ibid., 71.

72. Ibid., 83.

73. Webster, *Works of Daniel Webster*, 1:121.

74. Bancroft, *History of the United States*, 4:414.

75. Hart and Channing, *American History Leaflets*, 1.

76. Langguth, *Patriots*, 22.

77. Tudor, *Life of James Otis*, 90.

78. Ibid., 92.

79. Bell, *Personal Challenge*, 19–20.

80. Ibid., 21.

81. Galvin, *Three Men of Boston*, 48.

82. Sparks, *Library of American Biography*, 105.

83. Galvin, *Three Men of Boston*, 80.

84. Quincy, *Reports of Cases Superior Court*, 442.

85. Sparks, *Library of American Biography*, 120.

86. Ibid., 125.

87. Fritz, *Cast for a Revolution*, 76.

88. Ibid., 76–77.

89. Galvin, *Three Men of Boston*, 162–63.

90. Sparks, *Library of American Biography*, 170.

91. Galvin, *Three Men of Boston*, 179.

92. Menard, "Politics, Passions and the Law," 9.

93. Ibid., 10.

94. Ibid., 11.

95. Ibid., 12.

96. Ibid., 14.

97. Bowen, *John Adams*, 536.

98. *Boston Gazette*, May 26, 1783.

99. Galvin, *Three Men of Boston*, 175.

CHAPTER 6

100. *Hyannis Patriot*, July 4, 1929.

101. Lodge, Warren and Ford, *Warren-Adams Letters*, 1:2.

102. Zagarri, *Woman's Dilemma*, 15.

103. Richards, *Mercy Otis Warren*, 4.

104. Richards and Harris, *Mercy Otis Warren*, 3–4.

105. Ibid., 46.

106. Fritz, *Cast for a Revolution*, 130.

107. Ibid., 258.

108. Ibid., 267.

109. Ibid., 235.

110. Ibid., 269.

111. Cappon, *Adams-Jefferson Letters*, 1:107.

CHAPTER 7

112. Palfrey, *Discourse Pronounced*, 39.

113. *Niles' Weekly Register*, December 26, 1812.

114. Maclay, *History of American Privateers*, 468.

115. *Niles' Weekly Register*, July 10, 1813.

116. *Boston Saturday Evening Gazette*, August 24, 1861.

117. *Niles' Weekly Register*, July 10, 1813.

118. Blackington, "Mad Jack," 41.

119. *Connecticut Courant*, May 17, 1814.

120. Westcott, "Captain 'Mad Jack' Percival," 315.

121. Stevens, *Cruise on the Constitution*, 18.

122. *Niles' Weekly Register*, October 17, 1818.

123. *Journal of Lt. Charles Gauntt*, 4.

124. Torrey, *Journal of the Cruise of the United States Ship Ohio*, 21.

125. Hoyt, *Mutiny on the Globe*, 188.

126. McKee, "'Mad Jack' and the Missionaries," 35.

127. Hawthorne, *American Note-Books*, 91–92.

128. Melville, *White-Jacket*, 36.

129. Allen, *Papers of Isaac Hull*, 178.

130. Percival, Letter to Mahlon Dickerson, May 5, 1838.

131. Parker, *Recollections of a Naval Officer*, 137.

132. Dale, *Journal of J.B. Dale*.

133. Lynch, *Journal of D.H. Lynch*.

134. *Barnstable Patriot*, October 20, 1863.

CHAPTER 8

135. Chase, *Lemuel Shaw*, 3.

136. Williams, Letter to Reverend Mr. Shaw, March 12, 1784.

137. Chase, *Lemuel Shaw*, 6–7.

138. Shaw, Aldrich and Thomas, *Lemuel Shaw*, 5.

139. Chase, *Lemuel Shaw*, 25.

140. Ibid., 114.

141. Ibid., 136.

142. Ibid.

143. Harvey, *Reminiscences and Anecdotes*, 127–28.

144. Ibid., 127.

145. Agnes, "Supreme Judicial Court—1962–1992," 25.

146. Chase, *Lemuel Shaw*, 203.

147. Ibid., 161.

148. Ibid., 170.

149. Ibid.

150. Levy, *Law of the Commonwealth*, 26.

151. Butler, *Autobiography of Personal Reminiscences*, 1002.

152. Holmes, *Common Law*, 106.

153. Phillips, *Felix Frankfurter Reminisces*, 234.

154. *Barnstable Patriot*, April 5, 1915.

155. *Barnstable Patriot*, August 7, 1916.

156. Savage, *Lemuel Shaw*, 5.

157. Shaw, Note to Levi Goodspeed, March 29, 1815.

CHAPTER 9

158. *Barnstable County Records*, 9:214.

159. Dix, *Memorial to the Legislature of Massachusetts*, 2.

160. *Barnstable Patriot*, November 15, 1848.

161. *Barnstable Patriot*, January 11, 1853.

162. *Barnstable Patriot*, April 16, 1889.

163. *Barnstable Patriot*, May 21, 1889.

164. *Barnstable Patriot*, September 19, 1963.

165. *Barnstable Patriot*, August 11, 1913.

166. *Hyannis Patriot*, October 15, 1923.

167. *Barnstable Patriot*, March 17, 1927.

168. Ibid.

Bibliography

Adlow, Elijah. *The Genius of Lemuel Shaw.* Boston: Massachusetts Bar Association, 1962.

Agnes, Peter W., Jr. "Supreme Judicial Court—1692–1992." *Massachusetts Lawyers Weekly Special Section* (October 19, 1992).

Allen, Gardner W., ed. *Papers of Isaac Hull.* Boston: Boston Athenaeum, 1929.

Bancroft, George. *History of the United States, from the Discovery of the American Continent.* Boston: Little, Brown, 1856.

Barnstable County Records, 1696–1894. Vol. 9. Barnstable County Probate and Family Court, Barnstable, Massachusetts.

Bell, Hugh F. *A Personal Challenge: The Otis-Hutchinson Currency Controversy, 1761–1762.* Salem, MA: Newcomb and Gauss Company, 1970.

Blackington, Alton H. "Mad Jack." *Yankee* 25 (July 1961): 41.

Bowen, Catherine Drinker. *John Adams and the American Revolution.* Boston: Little, Brown, 1951.

Bradford, William. *History of Plymouth Plantation.* Edited by Charles Deane. Boston: privately printed, 1856.

Brown, Alice. *Mercy Warren.* New York: Charles Scribner's Sons, 1903.

Bullen, Ripley P., and Edward Brooks. "Shell Heaps on Sandy Neck, Barnstable, Massachusetts." *Bulletin of the Massachusetts Archaeological Society* 10, no. 1 (1948).

Butler, Benjamin F. *Autobiography of Personal Reminiscences. Butler's Book.* Boston: A.M. Thayer and Company, 1892.

Cappon, Lester J., ed. *The Adams-Jefferson Letters: The Complete Correspondence Between Thomas Jefferson and Abigail and John Adams*. Chapel Hill: University of North Carolina Press, 1959.

Chapelle, Howard I. *The History of the American Sailing Navy*. New York: W.W. Norton, 1949.

Chase, Frederic Hathaway. *Lemuel Shaw: Chief Justice of the Supreme Judicial Court of Massachusetts*. Boston: Houghton Mifflin, 1918.

Dale, J.B. *Journal of J.B. Dale, U.S. Frigate Constitution, 1844–46*. Boston: New England Genealogical Society, n.d.

Deyo, Simeon L., ed. *History of Barnstable County, Massachusetts*. New York: H.W. Blake, 1890.

Directors of the Old South Work, Old South Meeting-house, Boston, Massachusetts. Letter from John Adams to William Tudor. In *Old South Leaflets*, March 29, 1817, 179:4.

Dix, Dorothea L. *Memorial to the Legislature of Massachusetts*. Boston: privately printed, 1843.

Dunford, Fred, and Greg O'Brien. *Secrets in the Sand*. Hyannis, MA: Parnassus Imprints, 1997.

Dwight, Timothy. *Travels in New England and New York*. London: William Baynes and Son, and Ogle, Ducan and Company, 1823.

Ellis, James H. *Mad Jack Percival: Legend of the Old Navy*. Annapolis, MD: Naval Institute Press, 2002.

Ferling, John. *John Adams: A Life*. New York: Oxford University Press, 1992.

Freeman, Frederick. *The History of Cape Cod: Annals of Barnstable County*. Vol. 1. Boston: Geo. C. Rand and Avery, 1862.

Fritz, Jean. *Cast for a Revolution*. Boston: Houghton Mifflin, 1972.

Galvin, John R. *Three Men of Boston*. New York: Thomas Y. Crowell Company, 1976.

Gauntt, Charles. *Journal of Lt. Charles Gauntt aboard the USS Macedonian, 1818–21*. National Archives Microfilm Publication M875.

Goehring, Walter R. *The West Parish Church of Barnstable*. West Barnstable, MA: West Parish Memorial Foundation, 1959.

Gookin, Daniel. *Historical Collections of the Indians in New England*. 1st series, 1792. Collections of the Massachusetts Historical Society.

Grinnell, Frank W., ed. "James Otis, Jr., Oxenbridge Thacher and the Writs of Assistance 1761." *Massachusetts Law Quarterly* 38 (August 1953): 52.

Gross, Anthony, ed. *Lincoln's Own Stories*. Darke County, OH: Coachwhip Publications, 2007.

Hart, Albert Bushnell, and Edward Channing, eds. *American History Leaflets: James Otis's Speech on the Writs of Assistance*. New York: Parker P. Simmons, 1906.

Harvey, Peter. *Reminiscences and Anecdotes of Daniel Webster.* Boston: Little, Brown, 1877.

Hawthorne, Nathaniel. *The American Note-Books.* Boston: Houghton Mifflin, 1896.

Holmes, O.S., Jr. *The Common Law.* Boston: Little, Brown, 1881.

Hoyt, Edwin P. *The Mutiny on the Globe.* New York: Random House, 1975.

Kittredge, Henry C. *Barnstable, 1639–1939: A Brief Historical Sketch.* Hyannis, MA: F.B. and F.P. Goss, 1939.

———. *Cape Cod: Its People and Their History.* Boston: Houghton Mifflin, 1968.

Langguth, A.J. *Patriots: The Men Who Started the American Revolution.* New York: Simon and Schuster, 1988.

Levy, Leonard W. *The Law of the Commonwealth and Chief Justice Shaw.* Cambridge, MA: Harvard University Press, 1957.

Lodge, Henry Cabot, Winslow Warren and Worthington Chauncey Ford, comps. *Warren-Adams Letters.* Boston: Massachusetts Historical Society, 1917.

Lynch, D.H. *Journal of D.H. Lynch Relating to the Cruise of the Constitution Around the World, 1844–46.* N.p., n.d.

Maclay, Edgar S. *A History of American Privateers.* New York: D. Appleton, 1899.

Mallary, Peter T. *New England Churches & Meetinghouses.* Secaucus, NJ: Chartwell Books, 1985.

Maloney, Linda M. *The Captain from Connecticut: The Life and Naval Times of Isaac Hull.* Boston: Northeastern University Press, 1968.

Marshall, John. *A History of the Colonies of North America.* Philadelphia: Abraham Small, 1824.

Martin, Tyrone G. *A Most Fortunate Ship: A Narrative History of "Old Ironsides."* Chester, CT: Globe Pequot, 1980.

McCullough, David. *John Adams.* New York: Simon and Schuster, 2001.

McKee, Linda. "'Mad Jack' and the Missionaries." *American Heritage* 22 (April 1971).

Melville, Herman. *White-Jacket.* London: Richard Bentley, 1850.

Menard, Catherine. "Politics, Passions and the Law in Otis v. Robinson 1769." *Boston Bar Journal* (March 1983): 9.

Nye, Russell Scudder. *Scientific Duck Shooting in Eastern Waters.* Falmouth, MA: Independent Press, 1895.

Oldale, Robert N. *Cape Cod, Martha's Vineyard & Nantucket: The Geological Story.* Yarmouth Port, MA: On Cape Publications, 2001.

Palfrey, John G. *A Discourse Pronounced…At the Second Centennial Anniversary.* Barnstable, MA: S.D. Phinney, 1840.

Parker, Danl. *Order of the Justice of the Peace*, August 7, 1724. Private collection.

Parker, William Harwar. *Recollections of a Naval Officer.* Annapolis, MD: Naval Institute Press, 1985.

Percival, John. Letter to Mahlon Dickerson, May 5, 1838. National Archives Microfilm Publication M147.

Phillips, Harlan B., comp. *Felix Frankfurter Reminisces.* New York: Reynal and Company, 1960.

Powell, Bernard W. "An Archaeological Traverse of Sandy Neck, Cape Cod, Massachusetts." *Bulletin of the Massachusetts Archaeological Society* 28, no. 2 (1967): 4.

Province Laws (Resolves, etc.).—1717–18, 3rd Sess., Ch. 146. Province of Massachusetts Bay.

Quincy, Josiah, Jr., ed. *Reports of Cases Superior Court of Judicature of the Province of Massachusetts Bay, Between 1761 and 1772.* New York: Russell and Russell, 1969.

Richards, Jeffrey H. *Mercy Otis Warren.* New York: Twayne Publishers, 1995.

Richards, Jeffrey H., and Sharon M. Harris, eds. *Mercy Otis Warren Select Letters.* Athens: University of Georgia Press, 2009.

Ridpath, John Clark. *James Otis: The Pre-Revolutionist.* Chicago: University Association, 1898.

Sandborn, F.B., ed. *Familiar Letters of Henry David Thoreau.* Boston: Houghton Mifflin, 1894.

Schultz, Eric B., and Michael J. Tougias. *King Philip's War.* Woodstock, VT: Countryman Press, 1999.

Shaw, Samuel Savage, Peleg Amory Aldrich and Benjamin Franklin Thomas. *Lemuel Shaw: Chief Justice of the Supreme Judicial Court of Massachusetts.* Cambridge, MA: John Wilson and Son, 1885.

Shaw, Susanna. Note to Levi Goodspeed, March 29, 1815. Private collection.

Sinnott, Edmund W. *Meetinghouse & Church in Early New England.* New York: Bonanza Books, 1963.

Sparks, Jared, ed. *The Library of American Biography.* Boston: Charles C. Little and James Brown, 1848.

Stevens, Benjamin F. *A Cruise on the Constitution.* New York, 1904.

Stone, Edward C. "James Otis, Jr." Address, exercises, West Barnstable, Massachusetts, June 29, 1952.

Stowe, Harriet Beecher. *Oldtown Fireside Stories.* Boston: James R. Osgood and Company, 1872.

Swift, Charles F. *Cape Cod: The Right Arm of Massachusetts.* Yarmouth, MA: Register Publishing, 1897.

Swift, Charles F., ed. *Genealogical Notes of Barnstable Families Being a Reprint of the Amos Otis Papers.* Barnstable, MA: F.B. and F.P. Goss, 1888.

Swift, Charles W., and John D.D. Cogswell, comps. *Barnstable Town Records.* Yarmouthport, MA: Register Press, 1912.

Tapply, H.G. *The Sportsman's Notebook and Tap's Tips.* New York: Holt, Rinehart and Winston, 1958.

Teal, John, and Mildred Teal. *Life and Death of the Salt Marsh.* Boston: Little, Brown, 1969.

Thoreau, Henry David. *Cape Cod.* New York: W.W. Norton and Company, 1951.

Thygeson, H.E., comp. *Articles of Faith and Covenant of the Congregational Church, West Barnstable, Mass.* Hyannis, MA: F.B. and F.P. Goss, 1892.

Torrey, F.P. *Journal of the Cruise of the United States Ship Ohio in the Years 1839, '40, '41.* Boston: Samuel N. Dickinson, 1841.

Trayser, Donald G. *Report of Proceedings of the Tercentenary Anniversary of the Town of Barnstable, Massachusetts.* Hyannis, MA: F.B. and F.P. Goss, 1940.

Trayser, Donald G., ed. *Barnstable: Three Centuries of a Cape Cod Town.* Hyannis, MA: F.B. and F.P. Goss, 1939.

Tudor, William. *The Life of James Otis.* Boston: Wells and Lilly, 1823.

Waters, John J., Jr. *The Otis Family in Provincial and Revolutionary Massachusetts.* Chapel Hill: University of North Carolina Press, 1968.

Webster, Daniel. *The Works of Daniel Webster.* Boston: Little, Brown, 1853.

Westcott, Allan. "Captain 'Mad Jack' Percival." *U.S. Naval Institute Proceedings* 61 (March 1935): 315.

Williams, Abraham. Letter to Reverend Mr. Shaw, March 12, 1784. Private collection.

Zagarri, Rosemarie. *A Woman's Dilemma: Mercy Otis Warren and the American Revolution.* Wheeling, IL: Harlan Davidson, 1995.

Index

T

U

V

W

About the Author

J ames H. Ellis, a native of West Barnstable and a descendant of some of the leading first English settlers of Cape Cod, spent a career in government and civic affairs. A U.S. Air Force veteran of the Korean War, he graduated from the Honors College, Michigan State University. He headed the Crime Analysis Unit of the St. Louis, Missouri Police Department and worked as a management consultant for the International Association of Chiefs of Police. Ellis served as a senior staff member of good government organizations in Connecticut and Massachusetts and was chief of the Massachusetts State Police planning bureau. Later, he served in management positions with the U.S. Justice, Interior, Treasury and Labor Departments. He is the author of *Mad Jack Percival: Legend of the Old Navy* (2002) and *A Ruinous and Unhappy War: New England and the War of 1812* (2009), and he is a regular contributor to regional magazines and newspapers, as well as professional journals.